£1

MONEY TALK

By the same author

NO TIME FOR TEARS

MONEY TALK

A Lucrative Cocktail

SIDNEY BLOCH

BUCHAN & ENRIGHT, PUBLISHERS

LONDON

First published in 1986 by
Buchan & Enright, Publishers, Limited
53 Fleet Street, London EC4Y 1BE

British Library Cataloguing in Publication Data

Bloch, Sidney
   Money Talk: a lucrative cocktail
   1. Money
   I. Title
   332.4   HG221
   ISBN 0-907675-63-8

Typeset in Garamond in Great Britain by Leaper & Gard Ltd
Printed in Great Britain by Biddles Ltd, Guildford

IN MEMORY OF
Leonard Bloch FCA
A great brother and friend,
and a very remarkable accountant

CONTENTS

INTRODUCTION

When God created Adam, they had discussions about agriculture, animal breeding and family planning but they never got around to matters of finance. According to the Good Book, it took another twenty generations before anyone entered into a commercial transaction. The twenty-third chapter of the Book of Genesis reports a character known as Ephron the Hittite operating as an entrepreneurial property dealer. He sold Abraham the Patriarch a piece of land for four hundred shekels, a sum equivalent to the annual wages of some sixty qualified craftsmen at the time. Considering that the land — required as a mini-cemetery — was a small field in the middle of nowhere, Ephron was no mean operator.

Ever since that time, people throughout the world have slaved, bargained, fought, schemed, murdered, married and died for money. Both the Old and the New Testaments cite numerous examples of priests and prophets berating the masses for giving gold a higher rating than God; while, in Ancient Greece, in about 600 BC, the Sages reminded merchants that shrouds have no pockets. A couple of hundred years later, a wealthy aristocrat named Cephalus assured Socrates that the blessings of affluence enabled him to be generous and just — but nobody was convinced that money was entirely benevolent, Aristotle some time later stating that breeding money from money was unworthy of a free man, and Machiavelli, in the sixteenth century, claiming that to possess a fortune blinds men's eyes. More pragmatic but equally clear about the dangers of riches, Lord Chesterfield wrote to his student son in 1750, granting him an allowance sufficient to follow the pleasures of a gentleman — but not of a rake. (This still enabled the youth to have his own luxury apartment, his own carriage, and three servants.)

The fact remains that, throughout the ages, regardless of the wrath of God being poured down from the pulpits, money has survived as the most powerful of all tongues. In the persuasion stakes, Euripides, in the fifth century BC, had no qualms in backing cash against words. Holy and unholy wars have been financed by money extracted or plundered from the masses. Little children have been fed with materialistic dreams along with their mothers' milk, and greed has often driven the Faithful to crime. In his dissertation on the virtuous, Simon Cameron, a nineteenth-century American writer, declared that an honest politician is one who when he is bought, will stay bought.

This book is not about any of that. It is intended to be a light, informative and, I hope, amusing collection of money-oriented facts, figures, anecdotes and biographical sketches for the reader who enjoys browsing through familiar and less familiar facts about the world of money. Statisticians have claimed that no less than 189,999 textbooks have been written on the subject in the past twenty-five years. I have no way of checking the accuracy of this figure but, equally, I have no intention of making this the 190,000th. This is not an academic exercise or a guide for aspiring financial wizards. It is rather a money cocktail which I was encouraged to write, many years ago, by a very unusual man.

Humphrey K. Robinson was a roaming philosopher. He had neither capital nor income, but claimed the right to occupy a bench in a corner of Leicester Square within a hundred yards of a library. His laceless boots were several sizes too large for his feet, and a paper bag held all his worldly possessions. He had no respect for material assets and even less for those who valued them. His only aspirations were to read the Classics and survive without having to work. In my early days in business he agreed to answer the telephone in a public box near to his bench. It was the number which I gave to my potential clients. In return, I bought him lunch, which cost me two shillings a week. When I was able to establish my first, small office, he felt liberated from an onerous responsibility. Cautioning me to keep my values in perspective, he challenged me to write a dip-into money book — a modest exercise that might produce a smile, raise an eyebrow, provoke a thought, discourage the gambler, enlighten the naive and, above all, help to keep the value of money in focus.

It has taken me a long time to respond to the challenge but I am now happy to dedicate these pages to a rare knight of the road, Humphrey K. Robinson.

SIDNEY BLOCH
London 1986

THE QUESTION
OF MONEY

When it is a question of money,
everybody is of the same religion
Voltaire

First came simple bartering, then specific items were used to
exchange for whatever goods were desired — over the
centuries, precious stones, cattle, the jaw-bones of pigs,
tobacco, slaves, cowries, and numerous other commodities,
have served as money. Theological scholars have no doubt
that the Old Testament produced the earliest evidence of
hard currency in an exchangeable form, and Professor
Bender, an authority on the subject, spent some years earlier
this century strolling up and down the banks of the Nile and
the back streets of Athens before reaching the same conclusion; his research also showed that coinage, *per se*, dates
back to about 2000 BC. The actual word for money,
however, has its origin in Rome: following the Gallic
invasion of that city in 344 BC, Lucius Furino built a temple
to Juno; subsequently, the first Roman mint was erected in
the monument in order that the coins — called *asas* — might
come under the goddess's protection. The word 'money' is
derived from Moneta, a surname or title given to Juno — as,
indeed, is the word 'mint'.

In a bold but ultimately unsuccessful endeavour to
provide a precise definition, the economist Ralph Hawtry
stated that: 'Money is one of those concepts which, like a tea-
spoon or an umbrella, but unlike an earthquake or a buttercup,

are definable primarily by the use or purpose which they serve.'
The difficulty of arriving at a single, clear-cut definition has
led people to describe it variously as an instrument of
measuring wealth, a medium in which prices are expressed,
a facility for stating the value of possessions or property, and
a tangible form for creating a market or an exchange. It has
provided the means to finance armies and wars, acquire
prestige and sustenance, and buy influence, politicians and
friends.

Different from the money antics of individuals, are the
financial manipulations orchestrated by governments and
blessed by Central Banks, referred to as monetary policies.
These are technological theories activated to produce greater stability. The grandiose title carries a most convincing ring
but, in practice, the monetary philosophies of most states
produce a level of security comparable to an elevator with
an elastic cable. But, then, governments are composed of
politicians and statesmen, and where money is concerned,
they have often made strange bed-fellows. It is in the grey
area between state bureaucracy and individual ambition that
money has created power, fortunes and shame — possibly
the off-shoots of the monetary policies of governments
rather than of the financial gyrations of entrepreneurs, for
whom money is a challenge, a master, a quantifiable symbol
of success. Today, the talk is of credit cards as plastic money
which can bridge the gap between banks and home computers. Tomorrow, money could change its meaning if not its
purpose.

Values constantly change in terms of individual circumstances and demands. The contented, the discontented, the
ambitious, the gambler, the hungry and the dreamer — each
has his own formula for evaluating money. Few stop to
consider its rating in terms of legal tender for other values,
such as the quality of life or happiness; one of the most
fascinating and surprising aspects concerning the acquisition
of money is the fact that few of those setting out to make a
fortune realize that there will be a price to pay. Indeed,
many of those who have accumulated wealth have not really
appreciated just what it has cost them.

MILLIONAIRE'S ROW

Who and How and So What

> If all the rich men in the world divided up
> their money amongst themselves, there would
> not be enough to go round.
>
> *J. Bertillon*

In his excellent book, *It's No Sin To Be Rich*, William Davis expressed the view that the ability to concentrate is a most important ingredient in the formula for financial success. Others claim it is enthusiasm, a capacity for hard work or a determination to succeed. All these attributes could equally apply to a conscientious clerk who seeks little more than a reasonable salary, a modicum of recognition and sufficient leisure time to nurse his garden. Such men are often respected for their loyalty and live to a ripe old age. They never seek or experience affluence unless they happen to be the only surviving relation of a wealthy aunt.

In the domain of self-made millionaires, men probably have no more than three major qualities in common: flair, the ability to recognize opportunities and the capacity to exploit them. The methods they employ in achieving their objectives, however, differ, invariably reflecting a distinctly individual rather then stereotype style. Trusthouse Forte, the international hotel group, grew from a sandwich bar entirely through the efforts of a shrewd workaholic, Sir Charles Forte. On the other hand, an even larger enterprise, Grand Metropolitan Hotels, was built by an imaginative, unassuming ex-corporal, Max Joseph, who claimed that he never worked more than four hours a day. Nigel Broackes, who had some difficulty in finding his commercial feet, launched Trafalgar House largely on an inspired hunch and integrity, qualities which have continued to under-pin his vast conglomerate. Men like Onassis and Charles Clore were special-situation spotters dedicated to hard work. Billy Butlin, a jovial extrovert, recognized and filled a need for the working classes by pioneering a new class of holiday camp. Cuthbert Heath brought innovation to the Lloyd's insurance market, and Lord Marks, the greatest storekeeper of the century, concentrated on staff relations as he marketed quality. Robert Maxwell could best be described as a clever survivor, while Jimmy Goldsmith is a highly successful entrepreneur guided by flair. None of them acquired the dignity of Lord Samuel of Land Securities but their handshakes were, or are, all respected when it came, or comes, to a deal.

And so the list of millionaires continues to grow. Although few of the self-made had any real education, they all had street-sense, a gut-tuning that enabled them to amass fortunes. Others, frequently more polished, more sincere and better educated, settled for far less in material terms. There is, however, one experience shared by the majority of successful, first-generation innovators — men like Clore, Onassis, Maxwell and Vanderbilt — they all knew hard times, and proved that there's no incentive like an empty stomach. Sadly, many have shown a marked inability to achieve any real semblance of happiness in their lives. Both Onassis and Clore were utterly miserable in their last years, leaving behind them wealthy families to fight over their vast millions. To his credit, Clore, having made his children wealthy in his lifetime, left most of his fortune to charity under the benevolent guidance of his only daughter, Vivienne Duffield. John D. Rockefeller amassed around two hundred million dollars, and left behind a host of people who loathed him. When the oil king, Nubar Gulbenkian, died, a wit accurately predicted, 'The Ritz will mourn him longest.' Howard Hughes, one of the world's richest tycoons, died a recluse, friendless, childless and neglected. Stories of the punctured dreams of multi-millionaires have been underscored throughout the centuries back to biblical times. Even King Solomon, reputed to be the wealthiest man who ever lived, was deserted by his friends and his wives in his last years. Blamed for misfortune and havoc, his alleged virtues have always remained in doubt.

On the strength of the above it might well be argued that 'a happy millionaire' is a contradiction in terms, but fortunately there have been some who justify the description. While the prime aim of commercial millionaires continues to be to make money, and yet more money, the truly great artists become wealthy because they excel in their professions, and bring pleasure to many. Such people, who have made their fortune in the arts, have a better track record for humour and genuine friendships than the successful traders: Luciano Pavarotti, Bob Hope, Yehudi Menuhin and Pietro Annigoni, among many, have made their marks in their own worlds and still radiate a certain charisma that is rarely found among the barons in commerce. There are of course exceptions in the business world, too: among them might be numbered Lord Weinstock, the man who allegedly kept a smile on his face most of the time he was re-building the General Electric Company. Another was certainly Sir John Cohen, the East End barrow boy who built the mighty Tesco supermarket chain and managed throughout his life to combine a tough business stance with courtesy; when he died he left behind many good friends and numerous wonderful memories for his happy family. The diamond king, Sir Harry Oppenheimer, might well be similarly described, but then he is second-generation affluence — and it is usually so much easier for them to smile.

Some never own the empires they build; among these self-made professionals is Harold Geneen, the ex-mogul of ITT. In the early seventies, when he was about fifty years old, he received an annual salary of $1,000,000 with perks to match. He treated the company more like a religious order than a commercial enterprise and expected his minions to prostrate themselves before one god, Harold Geneen. Employing the principle of the golden handcuffs, he was able to attract the most able, ruthless manipulators and unscrupulous negotiators to his board. A faceless man with a

genius for intrigue, he was obsessed more with power than
with money. But it is doubtful if Geneen will be remembered beyond the bounds of his old company and those
who suffered during his reign.

With relatively few exceptions — Carnegie, Ford and
Clore, for instance — those who have amassed wealth tend
to be remembered more for their eccentricities and their
quips rather than their fortunes. Calouste Gulbenkian is
almost forgotten outside of the oil world despite the existence of a large trust in his name. His son, Nubar, however, is
largely remembered for having the gold-plating of his taxi
painted black as a sign of mourning for his mother. Willy
Vesty, a fun-loving millionaire, once declared honestly, 'I
have a brilliant brother, he spends his life making money for
me and I devote my days to drinking his health.' Lady
Docker, a glamorous bar-maid who married three millionaires, announced, 'Wherever I go, I am the cabaret.' John D.
Rockefeller, who gave away over $700,000,000 in his life-
time, made a large donation to the University of Chicago on
condition that it employed no 'infidel' teachers. (Although
this was known to refer specifically to Jews, it did not
prevent the governors accepting the gift.) The Rockefellers
have been described as having had everything except a
good name. Aristotle Onassis, in his determination to be the
greatest and marry the greatest, gave Jackie Kennedy
$3,000,000, and $500,000 a year, as a wedding present. That
did not discourage her from successfully claiming a further
$20,000,000 from Ari's estate only a few years later.

When asked by an aspiring yacht-owner how much it cost
him a year to run his boat, the banker, J.P. Morgan replied
bluntly, 'If you got to ask, you can't afford it.' Dan Guggenheim — who once declared that he stopped counting his
money after making the first $100,000,000 around the turn
of the century — and Bernard Baruch were together at a
party when their hostess asked them how they knew when
the market topped out. Guggenheim replied, 'I expect it to
go no more than ten per cent above my selling price.'
Baruch shook his head with a smile, 'When I sell, I sell,' he
said. 'I get no pleasure watching a share go down afterwards'
— implying that he always sold at the top of the market.

Perhaps one of the most remarkable in the money-club
was William C. Durrant. He made his first million dollars by
1905 and went broke in 1910. By 1915 he had bounced
back to become the owner of General Motors. He was nothing if not consistent, and by the year 1920 he had amassed
and lost $90,000,000. But he was not down. Four years later
he left the motor industry with $20,000,000 and started trad-
ing on the New York stock market. Just before the great
crash of 1929, William Durrant did two things. He sold out
every single share he had, realizing a sum in excess of
$100,000,000. A few days later, before leaving for Europe, he
told the President of the US that the crash would come
within two months. His warning was ignored. The crash
came. There is no record of what Durrant did with his
fortune.

James Chapman, the oil baron, although not known for
his happy temperament, left most of his $100,000,000
fortune to medical institutions. During his lifetime Chapman
rarely referred to his only son, who at the time of his death,
was forty-seven years old. In his will, Chapman senior left
him just $1,000 without comment. This was the item that
appeared largest in most of the newspapers at the time.

In the broader category of great wealth must surely be
included two unusual men who failed to receive the fortunes
to which they were entitled. The first was the greatest British
sailor of all time, Admiral Lord Nelson. Entertaining like a
millionaire as he swept the seas of Britain's enemies, he was
a pride and joy to his country and a blessing to Lloyd's
underwriters, who would happily have rewarded him with a
generous annuity for the millions he saved them. Now,
nearly two hundred years after his tragic death, the Nelson
Room at Lloyd's is a delightful and extravagant monument to
his memory. Yet in spite of the wonderful and romantic
stories which fill the archives, there is little mention of the
fact that when Nelson died at Trafalgar he was virtually
broke. Being prepared for such an eventuality when he
wrote his will, he left his mistress, Emma, Lady Hamilton,
and their daughter, to 'My Government for safe keeping'. A
noble if rather cheeky idea which should have worked, but
did not. After giving Nelson a Westminster Abbey funeral,

the British government refused their 'inheritance'. 'We have no department to deal with such bequests,' a minister pronounced; the Admiralty considered it highly improper that such a delicate matter should be referred to them; as would be expected, there was no policy at Lloyd's to justify a claim, and nobody thought of a whip-round. Emma, a rather unpopular lady, soon ran through the income left to her by Nelson and died in poverty and debt, her pleas for financial help ignored by governments and underwriters alike. Thus was society seen to extract its price for her adultery. In time, a magnificent column was' erected in Trafalgar Square in honour of the great mariner. Licences galore were granted for the manufacture of millions of miniature models, and hundreds of books were published on the battle and its hero. The real debt to Horatio Nelson was never paid.

The second example is quite different but also concerned the British government. This time it was during the Second World War, when it had to be acknowledged that the Germans had command of European air-space by virtue of their superior aircraft and trained manpower. The British were surviving largely on Churchillian rhetoric and the firm belief that God was on our side. The time for a miracle, destruction style, had arrived. It would have been considered positively blasphemous to imagine that German prayers were also ascending to heaven at the same time. In the midst of it all, Frank Whittle, a young officer serving with the RAF, invented the jet engine. Its contribution to winning the war could not be overestimated any more than can the fortunes which it made for British and American manufacturers. In the aviation market, money took on a new meaning and the name Whittle became synonymous with British genius. After the war came the moment of truth. His Majesty King George VI gave Whittle the knighthood to which he was entitled, but the British government treated the honour like a cash settlement. A hard, long and undignified fight followed. Eventually, with bad grace, the government awarded £100,000 to Sir Frank Whittle, the man who shortened the duration of the Second World War. The public failed to appreciate the injustice, but the American Secretary of State for Defense declared, 'I never realized that a British honour was worth around $5,000,000, give or take $100,000.'

Who should be put on the shortlist of outstanding millionaires? The task of choosing them on the basis of their innovative ability, or of their personalities would indeed be difficult. Apart from an ability to recognize fortuitous circumstances, relatively few possessed the intellect, the charm or the distinctive personality to qualify for inclusion in the pages that follow. Those who do might best be described as being among the unusual in their time.

Hetty Green

Money may not buy you friends, but it
certainly gives you a better class of enemy.
Anon

There are relatively few today who are familiar with the
names of men like Baruch or Zaharoff and other moguls of
their generation. Yet, nearly one hundred years after her
death, the name of Hetty Green continues to figure among
the victims of money sickness.

Feminine emancipation brought women into the man-
made worlds of medicine, engineering, law and aviation at a
time when the enfranchisement of women was considered
little more than a gesture. Considering that, in addition to
looks, personality, perseverance and ability, many women
are shrewder than men, it is surprising that so few have
excelled in the field of business. Just as well, some people
might well argue, if that meant that they had to be like Hetty
Green, one of the most avaricious skinflints of her sex.

Neither squalor, poverty nor adversity haunted the background of this disagreeable miser. Born in New Bedford,
USA, in 1825, the daughter of a wealthy, Bible-thumping,
hard-fisted shipowner, she is described by her biographer,
Boydon Sparks, as a bold, handsome girl whose face hard-
ened while she was still young. Others were less complimentary.

For all a penchant she showed for nursing and domestic
drudgery, Hetty Green was a money-grubbing self-centred
shrew. Despite her affluence, her miserliness extended even
to herself, and her dowdiness was a constant source of
embarrassment and distress to those who were obliged to
entertain her. (It is alleged that, as an eccentric middle-aged
millionairess, she wore newspapers in lieu of under-
garments, which she was too niggardly to buy.) She was as
mean in spirit as she was with money, and her acquaint-
ances were constantly amazed that someone with her ability

to amass considerable wealth should have a personality as vindictive as hers was.

Her money-making career began when, at the age of about twenty, she was given $1,200 by her father to spend on herself. Instead, she bought bonds which she rightly reckoned were cheap. She didn't look back. Her well-developed ability to pursue grievances stood her in as good stead as her shrewdness, enabling her to ruin anyone who attempted to compete with her questionable business methods. Second only to her passion to hate, was her love for her only son. Until she dispossessed her husband, one E.H.Green, her marriage suited her well. It gave her the satisfaction of motherhood and enabled her to exploit the marked ability of a successful speculator — her husband. Before they separated, he helped her to make over one million dollars from a single deal. This was in about 1865, the year that General Lee ended the American Civil War by surrendering, Dostoevsky wrote *Crime and Punishment* and Abraham Lincoln was assassinated.

Such news was unimportant to Hetty Green. She was busy buying property, mortgages and railway stock, always at a time when they were out of fashion. She kept neither office nor staff, and managed to recoup most of her bank charges by making use of their premises. There were many in the New York financial world who were obliged to cope with her bad manners and hysterics, and few had the courage to get rid of her as a client. Apart from her shabby, graceless appearance and her highly disagreeable manner, the trouble with Hetty was her money. Almost regardless of her, her money continued to pile up and the bankers continued to court her custom and tolerate her tasteless eccentricities.

Once, asked to explain the secrets of her success, she confided, 'I believe in getting in at the bottom and out at the top. I buy cheap and sell dear. I never buy what others are buying. I never buy stocks and shares. I don't trust dealers.' She was served well by her theories.

Fortune, too, served her well. As luck would have it, Hetty inherited a million dollars from her father. Shortly afterwards, she felt obliged to contest the will of a wealthy aunt. The good lady had died, leaving her niece the entire income on an estate of some two million dollars. This was not the problem: what concerned Hetty was the capital, and she was prepared to commit forgery, perjury and fraud to get it. The litigation that followed was vicious and prolonged, and gave the newspapers one of their best and nastiest stories of the year. Eventually, with remarkably bad grace, Hetty settled for a cash payment of $650,000 in addition to the income. 'If I had had a good lawyer, I could have got my fair share,' she said after the case.

This strange woman, this highly successful trader, remained obsessively mean throughout her life. She hated spending to a point where she actually sacrificed the leg of her only son. She genuinely loved the boy, and nursed him unselfishly day and night, but she loved money more. Rather than incur the cost of a competent physician, she travelled around the hospitals in rags, begging for medical assistance for her only child. Medical help came too late and the boy's leg had to be amputated.

Being a great deal kinder than most, the writer, H.G.Wells, attempted to explain this miserable megalomaniac by the standards of the world in which she grew up. Generously, he contended that Hetty Green was over-influenced by a community which held that indigence was more vulgar and graceless than any physical deformity. This was the dogma that guided the philosophy and the indiscretions of the rich in the nineteenth century and persuaded the poor to accept their lot with undue humility.

This grotesque, wily old woman, who carried her deeds and her securities around in sacks, died at the turn of the century, leaving over twenty million dollars. The world that made her what she was hated her.

Basil Zaharoff

It is well known what a middle man is: he is a
man who bamboozles one party and plunders
the other.

Benjamin Disraeli

In October 1850, Napoleon III ruled France, and the Turks
began another bout of indiscriminate Christian killing. In the
village of Mughla in Anatolia, Basileios Zacharias, later
known as Basil Zaharoff, was born into a family of Greek
peasants. They were harrowing times. The Turkish massacre
of members of the Greek Orthodox Church was as mindless
as their refusal to repatriate Hungarian prisoners of war who
were a burden on the state. Such was the philosophy of
those who sailed the Bosphorus at a time when Wagner was
composing *Lohengrin* and the Californians were busy dis-
covering gold. This was the world into which Basil Zaharoff
was launched, destined to rise from poverty to become a
power in many countries far from his birthplace. While
Baruch and Graham understood the stock market, and Getty
could smell oil a mile away, Zaharoff perfected the art of
manipulating governments.

Zaharoff's climb to the top began when an uncle took him
into his run-down business; the young man rebuilt the business, and became a partner. But his uncle then reneged on
their deal, and their partnership culminated in a melo-
dramatic court case in London. The uncle was shown to be a
liar, and Zaharoff was cleared of a charge of embezzlement
to return to Greece where he led a very chequered career
before becoming a salesman in fire-arms. When asked which
territory he would like to cover, he immediately replied, 'The
Balkans.' Those were his original geographical limits but his
ambitions knew no fences. On the grounds that their
country was under threat from Greece, he completed a multimillion-pound arms deal with the Turks, then, the ink on the
contract barely dry, he sold the same story, in reverse, to the

Greeks. Those were the days when good lies were stock in trade and rough justice was law. It was about the time that France and Britain sent troops into Mexico to enforce pay-ment of financial debts, while the Russians, at peace, were orchestrating pogroms to distract their peasants from the pangs of hunger.

The First World War found Zaharoff virtually in control of Vickers, one of the largest British armament manufacturers. There he was largely responsible for the sale of billions of shells and cartridges, hundreds of thousands of machine-guns and over five thousand aeroplanes. All in four years. With his commissions running into many millions of pounds a year, his business morals allowed him to sell arms without prejudice or loyalty. Those who knew him well always suspected that he would be honoured by whichever side won the war: in the event, King George V gave him a knight-hood and the French awarded him the Grand Cross of the Légion d'Honneur. In the House of Commons comments were bitter, one member referring to Sir Basil as 'the angel of death'. When someone questioned Zaharoff regarding his feelings about the vast numbers of British and German volunteers who died in the Great War, he commented wist-fully, 'Yes, it is the patriots who underwrite my profits.' There were indeed many on both sides of the Channel who hated the Greek and mistrusted his motives. It was alleged by those who knew that Lloyd George had reason to protect him, but there was little proof other than the silence of the Prime Minister when challenged to speak.

A man of mystery, to be feared and mistrusted, a sinister figure who toured the powerhouses of Europe, successfully selling rumours on which wars are fed, a brilliant expert on backstairs politics, a man of ambiguous intelligence and territorial greed, he had risen from the slums to control the destiny of nations and the souls of men. Like Midas, his immeasurable fortune brought him transitory glory, few pleasures and little peace.

With uncounted millions, and few, if any, friends, Zaharoff eventually retired from business to live in seclusion in a castle in Monte Carlo, where, with petty cash of £1,000,000, he rescued the local casino; he was not however, a great gambler at the tables, seeing it, rather, as an investment. Rumours had long existed that he had nurtured a deep love for an unknown woman for many years. At the age of seventy-five, he married a lady described as an old friend and he doted on her until she died a year later. He died some ten years after her, in 1936.

Bernard Baruch

I live by the Golden Rule: 'He who has the
gold makes the rules.'

Anon.

John Kenneth Galbraith, one of the best known economists
of our time, achieved fame as a lecturer, an editor, an
adviser and as the author of *The Affluent Society* and other
bestsellers. Few people realized that he excelled as a character assassin. In his unbelievably vain 558-page autobiography, *A Life In Our Times*, he found no room for Paul
Getty but he managed to malign his colleague and mentor,
Bernard M. Baruch, no less than forty-six times. Perhaps he
found it difficult to accept that a man with breeding could
also make a vast fortune. If for no other reason than that he
appeared so many times in such an uncomplimentary light
in someone's autobiography, it is surprising that Baruch is
not mentioned in the *Guinness Book of Records*. Sadly, the
great Galbraith, for all his eventful and successful life, was
never comfortable with genius, feeling more at home with
intellectual mediocrity and those who either needed or
flattered him. He never recovered from this malaise or
achieved the stature of Baruch. The latter may have been a
gambler in his day but he had a natural talent for making
lasting friendships and playing his cards with dignity.

The son of a German Jewish doctor who emigrated to
America, Bernard Baruch was born in 1870. His financial flair
and handsome appearance enabled him to amass a personal
fortune of over $35,000,000 by the time he celebrated his
thirty-fifth birthday in 1905.

Legend has it that Baruch began to plan his fortune when,
as a teenager, he took his first job as a clerk in a stockbroker's office. Within a fortnight he had persuaded a bank
manager to lend him ten dollars. He kept the bills in his
office drawer for a week and then returned the loan with
interest. With variations, Baruch repeated this little game

month after month until his credit-worthiness was rated at
$100,000. It was then, at the age of nineteen, that he
developed the following investment policy which was to
produce a vast fortune for his clients and himself. He generously offered the advice in the hope that those who listened
would muster the necessary self-discipline to follow it:

1   Do not speculate unless you make a full-time job of it.
2   Beware of waiters and barbers and anyone bringing
gifts of inside information.
3   Before you buy a share, find out everything you possibly can about the company, its management, its earnings
and its possibilities for growth. Then check its competitors.
4   Do not try to buy at the bottom and sell at the top. It
does not work, except for liars.
5   Do not expect to be right every time.
6   Take your losses quickly and cleanly.
7   Do not try to be jack of all investments. Stick to the
field you know best.
8   Do not buy too many securities. Better to have only a
few investments which can be carefully watched.
9   Never, never invest all your funds.
10 Always keep a good part of your capital in a cash
reserve.
11 If you have made a mistake, accept it immediately, cut
your losses as quickly as possible.
12 Re-appraise your investments regularly to see whether
political or economic changes have altered their
prospects.

Finally, Baruch would tell his clients to find out all they
could about those who actually ran the companies in which
they invested. He often recalled a time when he watched the
president of a major corporation raise the stakes in a lunch-
time poker game to $5,000 a card. The year was 1898.
Baruch swore that he walked straight out of the hotel and sold
every share which he and his clients held in that company.
'In my mind, there's a world of difference between a calculated risk and a gamble,' he announced.

A man with the personal touch, he was still a law unto

himself. Strangely but not devoutly religious, he refused to trade on the stock exchange on the Day of Atonement in deference to his mother. That token of respect once saved him a quarter of a million dollars, he often related when asked to express his personal beliefs. At the same time, he found it acceptable and tenable to take his Protestant wife to synagogue on the occasional Saturday and join her in church on Sundays.

Probably one of the cleanest and greatest financial manipulators of his time, Baruch rubbed shoulders with the Guggenheims, the Morgans and the Rockefellers, and became a much-envied adviser to successive US Presidents. In his autobiography, published when he was eighty-seven, he made no mention whatsoever of John Kenneth Galbraith, and — unlike the economist — referred to his mother and father, with deep respect, no less than fifty-eight times; on the other hand, however, he made just one brief mention of his only son, aged fifty-seven at the time, and an honourable man. He referred frequently to President Roosevelt, whom he served as adviser, friend and confidant, but he did not mention Eleanor, although he knew her at least as well. She had leaned on him extensively over many years, but he was aware that she never quite forgave him his Jewish background; typically, he was able to bury his pride rather than mention her overt prejudices.

A chance meeting with Winston Churchill in New York before the Second World War marked the start of a lifelong friendship. Churchill made several complimentary references to Baruch in his autobiography, and it is alleged that on his ninetieth birthday Churchill sat up in bed and said, 'How I wish Berny was here.'

Baruch died at the age of ninety-five. A man well recorded in American history, who had advised presidents, governments and tycoons, he did little for posterity and the destination of his millions remains a mystery.

J. Paul Getty

There are but two families in the world ...
the Haves and the Have-nots.

Miguel de Cervantes

While Benjamin Graham might well have been described as a lively intellectual with a streak of financial genius, Paul Getty was a very different character, a man besotted with money and the power that it created.

The son of a once penniless farm-boy who became a successful attorney and then went into the oil business, Paul Getty was numbered among the world's richest men. He made his first fortune by the age of twenty-three and promptly retired. Years later, he confessed that by that time he was already sufficiently rich to revel in idle luxury for the rest of his life. But Getty had the wrong temperament to retire young. The oil in his blood and in his nostrils proved too much for his equilibrium, and he was back in the jungle of the oil business before his twenty-fourth birthday.

Getty had a natural ability to syndicate successful oil wells, to understand oil-rigs and drilling problems and, above all, to recognize golden opportunities. In addition, he cultivated a poker face which some say helped him in his negotiations. He believed in oil but, above all, he believed in himself. Once, when, probably flippantly, he declared that the Almighty had helped him build his business, a fellow oil tycoon remarked, 'I never knew Paul believed in more than one God.'

In 1931, when bankers were wary and money short, he master-minded a deal requiring immediate cash of one million dollars. Despite his conviction that the proposition offered enormous potential, his co-directors, long on enthusiasm, were short on confidence. Getty had just passed his twenty-seventh birthday when he gave his personal cheque for the $1,000,000 and undertook to carry his colleagues. Within a year he had acquired control of Pacific Western, one of the ten largest oil-producing companies in the whole of California. Later, when several of the best lawyers and accountants in America failed to convince the Revenue that $20,000,000 was too much to pay on his father's estate, Getty took over the negotiations himself. In due course the duty was reduced to $10,000,000. 'It was worth the trouble,' he is said to have commented when congratulated on the result.

Absolutely devoted to his mother, he insisted on protecting her future when, in 1933, she transferred her company interests to him. 'We'll deal with it simply,' he told his lawyers, and sent her bank a cheque for $4,000,000. To his mother he wrote: 'Mother, do not stint yourself.' The good lady was already over seventy. The only person he truly loved, her death was the one devastating non-commercial emotional experience of Getty's life; many found it difficult to reconcile with his image the deep sorrow and loneliness he suffered when she died.

With all his ability and natural business flair, the man who became a multi-billionaire was usually quite incapable of discriminating between his emotional and his commercial priorities. His first marriage, at the age of twenty, had all the makings of a genuine love match, enhanced by the beauty of his bride and the size of his bank balance. But it was not long before the excitement of his growing empire conflicted with the responsibilities of married life. When the marriage broke up, Getty declared honestly, 'The fault was mine. No bright and attractive wife can enjoy playing second fiddle to an oil-rig.' Four further marriages were to follow the same pattern. Yet, contrary to his severe appearance, he craved affection; once it was his, however, it failed to amuse or flatter him. As a talented and gifted businessman, he had few equals and fewer friends; as an art collector, he was rated one of the shrewdest; as a parent, he genuinely aspired to being a doting father — but as a husband, he proved to be a selfish, insensitive failure. Perhaps it was the mark of the man that he did not attempt to gloss over this weakness in his autobiography, *My Life And Fortunes.*

Besotted with business and money at the expense of human relationships, his reputation in his old age was that of the wealthiest and meanest man in the world. In a Utopian world, he was asked, should the meek inherit the earth? Unsmilingly he answered, 'It's OK with me as long as I get the mineral rights.' In his magnificent home in Surrey, filled with the finest paintings and rarest antiques, he installed a number of girlfriends ... and a pay-phone. The latter discouraged his guests from making long-distance calls; they complained bitterly behind his back, but continued to accept invitations to his parties.

As he grew older, Getty became more an enigma than a legend, preferring to spend his time with some of his grandchildren rather than with his peers. His death in 1983 brought his twenty-six heirs close together for the first time in years. Not to weep and mourn but to spend nineteen months battling over his $4,000,000,000 estate. More than twenty lawyers had a field day representing the various Gettys, clamouring for their feuding clients' portions. The legal fees, which Paul would no doubt have queried, were never disclosed but his two favourite sons each received $750,000,000 tax free. After a number of bequests, the disfavoured offspring was awarded $3,000 a year!

J. Paul Getty I left few genuine mourners but he will certainly be remembered for his art museum, in Malibu, California, which is currently spending $50,000,000 a year on acquiring paintings.

Benjamin Graham

*The difference between failure and success is
doing a thing nearly right and doing it exactly
right.*

Edward Simmons

What would rightfully be expected from a man with three
broken marriages who finished his life with a French mistress taken over from one of his sons? Might he also be a
keen dancer, an able tennis player, an enthusiastic skier, a
lover of Greek and Latin, an avid reader of Marcus Aurelius,
Virgil, Goethe and Proust, a philosopher who secretly identified himself with Ulysses?

Benjamin Graham, who died in 1980 at the age of eighty-
six, was such a man. He could also well rate as one of the
century's greatest and most unusual gurus on portfolio
management. An intellectual in any society, he applied pure
mathematics and simple logic to achieve one of the greatest
profit records in the American world of investment for
capital growth. In 1920 he formed a small syndicate of investors prepared to follow his unique philosophy and grant him
a share of the profits. At one time he acted as investment
adviser for Bernard Baruch but Baruch considered his
charge of 20 per cent of the profit he made for his clients to
be excessive. The men were in any case very different,
Baruch revelling in the political limelight, while Graham
sought little recognition outside his own circle. Years later,
when, observing his outstanding performance, Baruch
offered him a substantial profit-sharing association, Graham
turned it down.

In practice, he produced phenomenal results for his
clients, even after taking a very realistic share of the profits
he made for them. Those were the days when one was lucky
to earn more than 2 per cent from deposit accounts and
government investments. Graham consistently produced an
average net profit of over 20 per cent for more than twenty
years and then returned the initial capital to his investors.

The simplicity of his approach is illustrated in the criteria to which he stuck throughout his business life. Basically, the gospel of Graham could be summed up in the following golden rules:

1 A share should only be bought at a figure less than two-thirds of its net, quick assets.

2 The company should owe less than it is worth and preferred stock should be treated as a debt. In this way no company which qualified for inclusion in Graham's portfolio would have borrowed more than the value of its own assets.

3 The earnings yield should be twice that of an AAA Bond yield — i.e. the return from the loan stock of a first-class company. If an AAA Bond yield was 5 per cent, Graham would only buy a share with a 10 per cent earnings yield.

4 Sell after the stock has risen 50 per cent and do not worry about additional profit which might still be in the share.

5 In any event, sell after two years.

6 Always sell if the dividend is omitted.

7 Always sell if earnings decline so that Criterion 1 is not met.

Some might argue with the wisdom or practicability of the Graham system. The fact remains that, in application, it has continued to maintain its performance. Quietly, one American firm has specialized exclusively in following the Graham Method throughout this entire period. Almost unknown, Tweedy Browne Incorporated have consistently followed the policy of the man who introduced it to their partnership more than sixty years ago. Sufficient to record that anyone who invested $100,000 with Tweedy Browne in 1960 would have been worth nearly $7,000,000 in 1986. In 1974, when the Dow Jones fell by around 34 per cent, TB still made a small profit. It is an amazing reflection of their modesty that a millionaire who wished to invest with the firm in 1982 had to telephone more than a dozen banks and stockbrokers to find someone who had ever heard of them. The ghost of Benjamin Graham still walks in Wall Street, and investors with Tweedy Browne bless his memory.

Laura Sloate

A sixth sense and a little luck is a good
formula for success.

Dorothy Parker

Wall Street can claim to have produced more success stories
than any other financial centre in the world. There is no
shortage there of evidence of businesses that grew from a
few dollars to vast corporations in the space of only a few
years, of men who built and managed multimillion-dollar
investment funds and yet failed to make news in the financial press. It is a world where a millionaire is judged as a
man who is holding his own rather than someone of affluence.

Typical of the attitude adopted by those who live in this
rarefied atmosphere, was a Wall Street broker who, when
asked why he did not include a particular client in his social
circle, replied, 'Well, the guy's perfectly honest and able. His
trouble is that he's worth around $10,000,000 but talks as if
he has real money.'

The overwhelming majority of Wall Street's millionaires
are male, and if Hetty Green were the only female example
worthy of mention in this area, women might well feel
happy to leave it to men to prove that the love of money is
the root of all evil. But the true story of Laura Sloate is a
veritable fairy story in a world where man eats man for a few
dollars. A failed law student, she was determined to make
her name in the field of money management. Her greatest
assets were her determination, her ambition and her flair.
While men like King Hussein of Jordan have a sixth sense to
warn them of personal danger, and 'Delfont can spot a star'
by the way she walks into a room, Laura has a gut feeling for
the stock market. There can be few fund managers who, at
the age of twenty-five, decide to sell all their investments on
the hunch that the market was about to reach the top. Laura
Sloate did just that and then, barely a year later, placed

millions of dollars of clients' funds straight back into the stock market. In both instances, her timing was perfect and her clients made substantial profits.

All this might add up to just another story of a lucky whiz-kid who kept her ear close to the ground and her eye on the ball. The only difference is that Laura is blind. Her guide dog Ora is her shepherd and constant companion, and she rightly claims that her remarkable memory is her greatest asset.

Before she was fifty, she controlled her own investment-management concern, employing over twenty people and handling close on a hundred million dollars in clients' funds. Over breakfast, each morning, members of her family would read her the financial sections of all major newspapers, giving her the facts, the figures and the opinions. The mini computer inside her brain did all the rest. Laura has never seen a balance sheet, a company report or a share certificate and yet she is able to speak at length on the progress and potential of hundreds of quoted securities.

There were times when her concern to succeed at all costs made her less than popular. Some described her as just a little too self-confident; others, less subtle, claimed she exploited her blindness to get people's support and sym-pathy. It was probably all part of an aggressive determina-tion to prove that blind people may be disabled, but they are not handicapped. Today, she has mellowed, and her success has brought her the respect of her peers and the gratitude of many institutional and private clients.

A strange insight to her character was given when she was asked if she would take advantage of a miracle operation to restore her sight if such were possible. 'I do not know,' she replied. 'It would need a great deal of adjustment and I'm not sure that I would want to adjust.'

What of the Progeny?

Gentility is what is left over from rich
ancestors after the money has gone.
John Ciardi

In the minds of most beneficiaries, the divine right of kings
is extended to embrace the descendants of the affluent. Such
individuals accept their inheritance, confident that it will not
prove a handicap to their happiness. But unlike many they
sought to emulate, the children of the rich have often shown
a marked inaptitude to cope with responsibility and self-
indulgence simultaneously. They have mostly excelled in the
latter, content in the belief that their remarkable ability has
been adequately illustrated by their choice of parents. In
practice, there is overwhelming evidence to the contrary.
With notable exceptions like the Du Ponts, the Fords and
the Hoares, the scars created by inherited wealth rarely heal
before the assets are dissipated. The complexes and
neuroses which successful entrepreneurs produce in their
children have launched more psychiatrists than any founda-
tion. This fact no doubt encouraged William Kauffman, in his
book, *Emotional Uses of Money*, to make reference to
'Money sickness being clinically evident among those
disturbed by excessive wealth ...'

The theory is wonderfully illustrated by George W.
Vanderbilt, a grandson of the great Cornelius, who achieved
hereditary success at the age of twenty-six. Recognizing an
occasion for celebration beyond the normal reaches of self-
indulgence, he built himself a French renaissance château in
twelve thousand acres of land. This two-hundred-and-fifty-
room palace was reached by a three-mile illuminated drive
lined with over five hundred varieties of flora. Estimates of
the total cost of this extravaganza vary between seven and
ten million dollars, including the landscaping. The year was
1895. The building was completed and the lawns finally

manicured in time for its opening to coincide with one
hundred years of Vanderbilts. It was also the thirteenth
anniversary of the abolition of slavery in the US. At that time,
freedom was bringing the average black American $5-$10 a
week.

One still hears of the Vanderbilts in societies where rever-
ence for the Almighty has been replaced by worship of the
Golden Calf. Other great château-builders, like Flagler, Deer-
ing and Hubert Parson boarded the same bandwagon, but
prosperity barely records their opulent imitations. It is a
small comfort to the poor that ostentation breeds its own
disenchantment, and conscience drives a minority of pluto-
crats to benefit society. Among those remembered in this
exclusive group are Morgan, Frick, Carnegie and the odd
Rockefeller who converted their residences into libraries and
museums. What most of the tycoons lacked in culture and
art appreciation, they made up in shrewd tax-planning.
Under American tax law, a gift to a centre of learning was tax
deductible almost regardless of its real or imaginary value.
Who was there to argue that a Rembrandt purchased for
$100,000 might not be worth three times that a year or two
later? In this way a man with an income equivalent to the
value of the gift could avoid tax altogether. There were few
curators or connoisseurs with sufficient means or confidence to question guessed-at valuations backed by hard
cash. In the 1970s, the IRS estimated that works of art
presented to museums had been valued at $5,725,000. Their
actual cost had barely topped $1,500,000. Unlike entre-
preneurial zeal and a veneer of good manners, the ability to
defraud the Revenue was often congenital. It came with the
inheritance, and was frequently entirely responsible for
preserving great wealth for several generations.

According to reliable business magazines, the top
hundred US corporations are still governed, or substantially
owned, by the families of the original founders. The proud
boast does not include any executive commitment. In the
UK the record shows that the descendants of the great are
even less inclined to grace the boardrooms of the companies founded by their recent ancestors. Names like Mond
(of ICI), Dunlop, Montague, Warburg, Morris, or Portal

barely ring bells of recognition in the corridors of the empires they launched.

There are many who continue to wonder why so few large businesses ever make or survive the third generation. Randolph Hearst, the newspaper tycoon, Dewar of the distillery, Onassis with his shipping fleet, and countless others, had one thing in common apart from their wealth: their sons, grandsons or sons-in-law were not disposed to follow their examples, and, more regrettable and surprising, few of these offspring excelled in other fields. Men able to build empires and vast fortunes all too often lacked the time or the know-how to inspire their children to share their ambitions or their values. Autobiographies consistently illustrate the priorities of those who equate family trusts with paternal responsibility and affection. Armand Hammer, the remarkable head of Occidental Oil, who, at the age of eighty was still working sixteen hours a day, serves as an excellent example: the autobiography of this secretive multimillionaire-connoisseur-philanthropist makes constant reference to his friendship with presidents, kings, politicians and giants in industry — but his only son is mentioned just once, and then merely with reference to a murder of which he had been found innocent.

Some might rightly ask whether many tycoons are so besotted with their success, and absorbed with their egos, that they unintentionally place their children on the periphery of their lives. Or, is it more likely that many of the sons of the moguls are merely utterly bored, disillusioned and uninspired by the conversation and style that became the hallmark of their fathers, and that this often gives them a neurotic or socially unacceptable attitude to their possession of fortunes? It is understandable that secure luxury can inhibit innovative thinking, that over-indulged children of all ages can resent their parents — but what fills the gap? Sadly, so many have become unable to distinguish the difference between the inanity of useless existence and the joy of graceful idleness. Living in this vacuum, it is not surprising that third-generation affluent drifters invariably leave little more than a name on a tombstone.

It would be quite incorrect to give the impression that

none of the great family businesses have been able to temper their success with a worthwhile and lasting code of behaviour. They are in the minority but one of the most out-standing must be the Rothschilds. After two hundred years of uninterrupted achievement, their secret could hardly any longer be memories of poverty or, latterly, even ambition. Perhaps it is family pride, the satisfaction and excitement of perpetuating a great name with a world-wide reputation.

More than a hundred years ago, the Rothschilds were already entrenched in the British aristocracy. They had their beautiful homes, their stables and their magnificent town houses. They entertained lavishly and, while retaining their own identity, enjoyed the company and the confidences of Royalty. Apart from their faith, they have been distinguished in two other areas which set them apart from certain of their peers. First, their charitable endeavours, for which the Roths-childs have been famed ever since the family came to England in the eighteenth century — a generosity towards the poor and less fortunate for which they have continued to be known through successive generations, and apart from countless individuals, there is hardly a worthy cause in the land that has not benefited from one or more members of the Rothschild family. Charity is not just a habit with them, it is part of their creed. Legend has it that when, as an old man, Nathan Myer Rothschild, the founder of the British side of the family, was asked what he considered his greatest personal achievement, many expected him to refer to his sons, his family or his bank. He didn't. He answered, 'I do not believe I have ever knowingly turned away from a person in need.' It was a proud boast, and one to which he was entitled.

The other distinction is in a rather different category. Unlike others who made their fortunes in the City, the Rothschilds rarely joined the jet-setting spendthrifts who spent their lives and family fortunes oscillating between the beds of St Moritz and those of the Côte d'Azur. Could there be a relationship between family standards, charitable endeavour and the true strength of a great dynasty? Or is the answer more elusive? Perhaps the new generation of Roths-childs, no longer so close to the practices of their faith, will show whether or not they are still sufficiently well-geared to perpetuate the family reputation. It is to be hoped that the pressures and influences of the later part of the twentieth century will not be a watershed for them.

ROGUES' GALLERY

Those Who Got Away
(AND ONE WHO DIDN'T)

Do not rely on strangers to steal from you.
Friends do just as well.

Giorgio Getcelli

It might be true that the devil has all the best tunes, but there are few who can play them as well. Historically, the non-violent criminal classes have fallen into two categories — the scheming rogues who sell greed and hope in the form of bogus investments, and the rest who steal, embezzle and cheat with less sophistication.

In the interests of social science, history and money, numerous learned tomes have been written on the criminal, his chemistry and his motivation. For many years these were produced by lawyers and non-fiction writers claiming to understand the driving forces behind gangsters and law-breakers. Their case histories were often intriguing and varied, but, with monotonous predictability, the authors all drew the conclusion that the criminal was an anti-social evil deserving of little tolerance and even less compassion. Punishments meted out were often in keeping with an unwritten formula consistent with the whims and prejudices of the period. This was the case until psychiatrists and psychologists entered the field and began analysing those who found the underworld their natural milieu. Once this form of theory and research had gathered support, medical science added a new dimension to law: the art of verbal defence in gaining sympathy by pleading mitigating circumstances. It was not long before the ruthless, gun-slinging, bank robber, who was once hanged in the market-place, was presented as a sad example of a deprived youth unbalanced by his early experiences. Such original theories were absolutely illuminating for imaginative medical students; and they were pure gold-dust to criminal lawyers. Untrumpeted and almost unannounced, a new industry was born. Books on serious crime and mental disorders began to change their emphasis and a new breed of medical writers happily allowed their imagination to run riot with their professional knowledge. Herb Goldberg, in *Money Madness*, refers to a 'misunderstood' character who really held all the aces and blamed his attitude to society on distress caused by his enlightened doctor-parents who openly discussed sex and violence when he was a child but retreated behind closed bedroom doors to talk about money. Such evidence, emotionally expressed, is almost guaranteed to move the sympathy of jurors from the victim to the accused.

It follows that any top-ranking professional criminal, appreciating the value of a survival kit, will include a psychiatrist on his pay-roll. There is nothing like a long track-record of neurosis to increase the confidence of a defending counsel. Maundy Felling, an American criminal escapologist, caught and convicted after having been on the run for twenty-five years, declared, 'All I ever needed was a couple of tools, a bent psychiatrist and a good bail-broker. Just my luck I had to find myself a lousy lawyer.'

Those who treat crime as an art, a challenge or a profession frequently ignore the element of luck essential to their success. Although many consider that being caught is an occupational hazard, or an exaggerated risk, discounting the role of the outside chance has often been their downfall. In common with legitimate business, insufficient attention to detail tends to distinguish the professional from the amateur. When Joe Bowers, a small-time crook, was caught robbing a store of $16 in 1936, he could reasonably have expected a three-year sentence. Unfortunately for Bowers, he had failed to notice that the store housed a post office. This made his hold-up a federal offence and he was sentenced to twenty-five years — five times the term that an embezzler of $250,000 was given in the same court.

Al Capone

To denigrate sin, we immortalize our
criminals.

Oscar Wilde

From a world of waste and void, the Almighty, in his
wisdom, created the earth and perpetuated His Name. Sadly,
the film world frequently does the same for the dregs and
miscreants of society. But for Hollywood, it is doubtful if the
notorious Italian-American gangster, Al Capone, would still
be remembered. He remains the foremost product of the
early Mafia period in the American crime world, the most
successful operator of his time in the fields of vice, bribery,
gang warfare and degradation.

Born in 1895, Capone was quickly recognized as a child
prodigy in the Italian arena specializing in illicit trading and
violence. He arrived in Brooklyn as a youngster, and it took
no time at all for his mentors to appreciate his natural enthusiasm for crime. Rising quickly through the ranks of low-
grade pimps and mean bouncers, he soon graduated as a
talented hit-man, before settling down to mastermind his
own business. In record time he established himself as a
power in the boot-legging trade, claiming more police on
his payroll than the average New York precinct. An acknowledged specialist in structuring and administrating brothels
and gambling saloons, he was an impatient man when it
came to negotiating territories with his competitors. He
simply liquidated them.

With the FBI on his trail, Capone moved to Chicago
where the underworld greeted him with a mixture of respect
and suspicion. Determined to build his reputation without
the formalities and niceties sometimes followed in his
profession, he politely made an early appointment to call on
his rivals. In recognition of his reputation, they all assembled
together to spell out the terms on which Al would be a
welcome member of the fraternity. Drinks were flowing fast

by the time Capone and his friends arrived, disguised as policemen. Before they were even recognized, every senior member of the Chicago mob had been gunned down. Capone's well-laid alibis were foolproof, and there were no prosecutions.

Capone, known to spend a million dollars a year on bribes, brought his own style to the underground world of the city. Nobody argued; the gangster prospered. In the year 1924, when the President of the United States had his salary raised to $75,000, Capone, then aged twenty-nine, had a tax-free annual income of $5,000,000. This came purely from his investments in prostitution and boot-legging. With a high desire for power and a low regard for life, he moved into gambling clubs and dog-tracks. This profitable diversification was skilfully achieved with the assistance of gun-happy hoods and well-greased palms.

A few years after arriving in Chicago, Al Capone, fearing for his life, successfully sought a jail sentence in order to hide from a rival gang. His well-carpeted cell contained such luxuries as comfortable furniture, a telephone, a ticker-tape and a radio. In addition, he was granted unlimited visiting privileges and was afforded every facility to conduct board meetings in his prison. Capone was buying rather than serving time. For several years this was the technique that he employed to protect his neck without losing control of his empire.

Although he was credited with hundreds of murders, the FBI succeeded only in charging him with tax evasion of relatively modest sums. When he was sentenced, the police tried to even the score as best they could: expressing real and imaginary fears that the gang-leader's friends might organize his escape, they arranged for the arch-criminal to be transferred from a State penitentiary to Alcatraz, the top-security island jail off the coast of San Franscisco. This time there were no special privileges. There was nothing to buy in cell 84, the eight-by-six-foot stone-floored apartment which became his new home. Even long-serving inmates like Machine-Gun Kelly and Creepy Karpowicz were not looking for his leadership or friendship. During his four and a half years there, Capone caused his jailers little trouble, and, after being hospitalized for months, he was released to live in style on his luxury estate in Florida. There, at the age of forty-eight, he died quietly of syphilis. The secrets of his vast fortune were buried with him.

Of such stories, films and cynics are made.

Spaggiari and Wilmott

Imaginative men follow different roads to the
same destination.

Giorgio Getcelli

In the records of big-time bank robbers, Albert Spaggiari will
always enjoy a place of distinction. A fearless soldier and an
outstanding escapologist, it was his exceptional planning
ability that brought him respect from Interpol, envy from his
peers, and a vast fortune. Known to be the brain behind the
$50,000,000 bank raid on the Société Générale in 1976, he
and his well-trained accomplices worked their way through
the sewers of Nice to bring off their coup. With the dedica-
tion and determination which greed can generate, the men
sweated night and day in the mire, building a twenty-four-
foot tunnel into the bank vaults. This was no 'try and see'
exercise: Spaggiari had a detailed map which showed the
precise position of every box and vault on all floors of the
bank; nothing was left to chance or imagination, and in due
course the team reached the room which housed the most
valuable possessions deposited in the bank. As a textbook
exercise in crime, it was faultless. Unfortunately, unexpected
rain suddenly threatened to flood the tunnel and the man
responsible for emergency situations gave the alarm. Without word or panic, Spaggiari led the escape through the
sewer in specially prepared rubber dinghies. But for this
piece of bad luck, the haul might easily have been
$100,000,000 rather than half that figure.

The troubles were not over. A freak tip-off brought about
the arrest of Spaggiari and his companions, and the story
made the headlines in most of the world press. Taking all
the credit for bringing the genius crook to justice, the
French police were only allowed to enjoy their glory for a
short time. After calmly and honestly disclosing all the facts
to his interrogators, Spaggiari implemented his personal
emergency plan and escaped; he was later learnt to have left

France with his share of the fortune, estimated at $10,000,000. Soon rumours were pouring into Interpol of sightings of Spaggiari, in various disguises, in most of the capitals of the world. They were all followed up, and they all led nowhere. The 'Master' had disappeared, leaving no trace, and he has not been heard of since.

Spaggiari's escapade, although a major success in its field, must still rank among those that required planning, nerve and endurance rather than just cheek and ingenuity. The case of Henry J. Wilmott III, a very different type, serves to distinguish between a daring thief and an inventive crook.

The case, also in the 1970s, of Henry J. Wilmott III, a successful American grain-merchant, received very little publicity. For it all happened in Switzerland and the Swiss hate publicizing anything that might tarnish the excellent reputation which their banks enjoy.

Shortly after arriving in Zurich, Henry Wilmott opened an account at one of the major banks with $100,000 in cash. He arranged to draw $500 a week, explaining to the manager that he settled most of his accounts with an American Express card. In this way, he left the distinct impression that his withdrawals would be purely petty cash, which, indeed, they were. Over the next few months, Wilmott entertained the bank manager several times at the fashionable Bauer Lac Hotel and freely discussed his American business interests. These relaxed luncheons also gave the bank manager the opportunity to talk about the services which the bank might provide in connection with Wilmott's international grain business.

One day, Henry casually mentioned that he had several million dollars' worth of US shares which he had in mind to deposit in the bank for safe-keeping, the idea being that if anything happened to him, his three children would have substantial assets outside the United States. 'These shares are strictly family investments,' he repeated several times. This information was music to the ears of the bank manager, who readily offered the security of the bank's famous vaults. Wilmott accepted the offer although, secretly, he thought the charge was on the high side. A period of several weeks elapsed before the parcel of share certificates was delivered, together with his signature and those of his three children. In return, the bank issued a receipt for shares which, on that day, had a value of $3,827,340. It was clearly understood that, in his lifetime, Wilmott could demand the securities but, in the event of his death, they belonged to his children in equal parts. He emphasized so often the importance of money being available to his children, that the manager specifically noted it in his report to head office.

Not long afterwards, Henry Wilmott opened a second account with the Geneva branch of the same bank. He told the manager that he was currently negotiating a multimillion-dollar grain deal with a local trader of the highest reputation, and asked if, in the strictest confidence, the bank could possibly confirm the financial standing of his intended part-ner. This presented no problem, as the man concerned was well-known throughout Switzerland for his wealth and integrity. As anticipated, the bank produced a glowing refer-ence which was duly presented to Henry for a modest fee. It was all handled with typical Swiss confidentiality. Under-standably though, when Wilmott subsequently requested a one-million-dollar overdraft for the deal, the bank politely but firmly insisted on security. The fact that the proposed loan was for a period of only four months made no differ-ence. The bank required cover for the loan.

Explaining that it was strictly a personal transaction and not one connected with his American enterprise, Wilmott offered his large share portfolio in Zurich as collateral. A smile returned to the face of the bank manager and instruc-tions were given for the appropriate documents to be prepared. As it was a short-term loan, the bank agreed that the shares could remain in the Zurich branch, but temporar-ily assigned to Geneva. In this way Swiss banking etiquette was maintained, with each branch earning either a fee or interest. In due course, the loan agreement for $1,000,000 was signed by all parties concerned. The Geneva branch had the written confirmation from Zurich that they were holding the uncharged share certificates, and Henry withdrew the full amount of the loan soon after the ink was dry. It was a neat and uncomplicated transaction with which all con-

cerned were more than happy. The interest on the loan had
been a small bone of contention but Henry had graciously
conceded a quarter per cent more than the deal was worth.
As fitted the occasion, he took the bank manager to the
Hotel du Rhône for lunch and chose a particularly fine bottle
of wine.

Three months later, the bank wrote to their customer
reminding him that the loan was due for repayment in
twenty-eight days. There was no acknowledgement. A
second letter mentioned that, under the terms of their agreement, the bank was legally entitled to sell Wilmott's securities if the loan was not paid within seventy-two hours of the
due date. When this registered letter was returned marked
'unknown', the Geneva bank manager wasted no time in
instructing his Zurich colleague to sell. This signalled a large
black cloud to fall across the Bahnhofstrasse and descend
into the boardroom of the bank's head office. Directors
were summoned, doors were locked, and clerks were sworn
to secrecy. The shares deposited by Henry J. Wilmott III
were intact — but they were all counterfeit. Telexes to the
registrars of General Motors, IBM and the Prudential confirmed their worst fears.

With the benefit of hindsight, it was perfectly simple. The
Geneva manager had rightly trusted the Zurich manager.
The latter had never felt obliged to check the certificates as
he was only holding them in trust. The Geneva grain
merchant, a most honourable man, had never heard of Henry
Wilmott. In due course it was discovered that there had been
a merchant in Chicago of that name but he had died a year
earlier. The gentleman using his name had disappeared into
thin air, but not before withdrawing all but $100 of his orig-
inal deposit.

Both Henry Wilmott and Albert Spaggiari avoided capture,
the former by planning nearly four months' grace before his
crime could be discovered and the latter by practising the art
of escapology he had mastered in the Organisation de
l'Armée Secrète. Without public announcements being made
by either country, the Swiss amended their bank loan procedure and the French tightened up their prison security.

Eamon O'Shea

Honesty is the best policy after making
money.

Sydney Thompson Dobell

In a two-roomed slum in the backstreets of Dublin, an
amateur midwife delivered the youngest of the eight children of Theresa and Thomas O'Shea. The year was 1910.
The soup kitchens of the neighbourhood had long been
providing the O'Shea family with most of their meagre diet,
unemployment and a large family having turned Thomas
into a marathon beer drinker and a petty criminal. He never
graduated to a level of making crime a profitable vocation
and was poorly rated by his professional colleagues. The
baby Eamon was destined for better things but none could
have guessed the route he was to take to achieve them.

A bright child, he excelled in arithmetic and what was
then known as 'Observation and Intelligence Tests'. At the
age of twelve he ran away from home; three years later he
was wanted by the police of three counties. Tipped off by a
friend, he avoided capture by taking a night boat to Liver-
pool where he established a small practice as an alibi expert.
Unfortunately for Eamon, an ungrateful client squealed on
him and he was obliged to make his way to London in a
hurry.

Little did he realize then that Providence was guiding him
along the path to luxury. It was in the big city that he bought
a fellow countryman a couple of beers in return for the
secrets of the three-card trick. Eamon practised for ten hours
a day for a week before challenging the customers of a
public house in Bow in East London. Unlike other card-
sharps, he allowed his clients to win more often than they
lost, achieving his profit by winning most of the games
where the stakes were high. Eamon was a popular customer
at the pub but he was far too ambitious to stay indefinitely in
such a poor district. Now an expert in his field, he

descended on the West End of London with the tools of his
trade and a smart, new suit. The money rolled in and Eamon
took himself a bride from among the good-looking wait-
resses at the Trocadero restaurant. Patsy was a pretty, bright-
eyed, no-nonsense girl who once declared, 'Eamon was the
type of man I was looking for. I was bored with virginity at
the time.'

By the mid-thirties, Eamon operating from a street stall in
all weathers, had an income several times that of Neville
Chamberlain, the Prime Minister. The business began to
worry Patsy. Not on moral grounds but because the incle-
ment weather was giving her husband a chesty cough and
she was convinced that he would develop tuberculosis.

Times were changing fast. Mussolini was taking Italy into
Abyssinia and Hitler was planning to use his Austrian base to
invade Czechoslovakia. Politicians in England were scream-
ing about guns and war and the means to discourage the
German advance across Europe. 'With your brains, you
could go into the munitions business,' Patsy told Eamon.
She was right. But Eamon was determined to apply the
principles of the three-card trick, rather than the philosophy
of Zaharoff, to succeed in his new business.

Posing as an agent for the government, he quickly gained
the confidence of leading arms manufacturers who were
hungry for orders. Having ascertained their production
potential, he would then approach the War Office and Minis-
try of Supply in the guise of an arms manufacturers' representative. His gimmick was to guarantee profit margins for
the duration of the war. When the arms manufacturers
expressed some concern at the terms of the contract he
answered happily, 'You get over the problem by cheating.
All you have to do is to declare that your raw materials are
costing you more.'

Nobody complained. In addition to his commission from
the arms manufacturers, Eamon demanded and obtained
two per cent in cash to cover alleged bribes to government
officials; by the time Chamberlain got around to declaring
war, this had risen to five per cent.

Within a few years, every major bank and safe deposit
company in London had a security box rented by Eamon

O'Shea, who now lived in one of the better West End hotels where the staff treated him and Patsy like royalty. Eamon was determined not to be too greedy and paid many thousands of pounds of tax on his commission income. The bribery fees he hid. At the end of the war, he was faced with the serious problem of legalizing over a million pounds in cash. With his ear close to the ground, he soon learned of most of the 'washing' schemes that were available. These mostly revolved around injecting black-market money into bogus companies which later went into liquidation. The distribution of assets gave the shareholders their original capital less fees and discounts varying between ten and thirty per cent. One would have to think of a much brighter plan today to convince the revenue authorities. After discussing the risks involved, he and Patsy decided that they would have to evolve their own plan. The idea of trusting faceless middlemen did not appeal to them.

In 1947 Eamon visited Eire. Years later he confided to a bent police inspector in the Colonies that he had gone there to buy a lawyer. This professional gentleman was to become a specialist in the 'inheritance scheme', the brainchild of Eamon O'Shea. The secret of the exercise was not to hurry, but to watch the obituary notices for the deaths of rich Englishmen living abroad. In due course, the lawyer learned that a wealthy colonel had died and been buried in Gibraltar. It was not long before a simple will was forged which left Eamon a substantial sum. The usual advertisement seeking the whereabouts of one Eamon O'Shea, who could learn something to his advantage, appeared in the London *Times*. Eamon replied, and later forwarded a copy of his birth certificate, provided by the lawyer. With the help of a tame accountant, feeding the cash in and out of the lawyer's client's account presented no problem. Over a period of two years Eamon was to learn that he was a beneficiary under the wills of a number of his wealthy 'relatives'. When he and Patsy arrived in Jamaica, where they settled, they deposited large cheques in two British and two Canadian banks. Half their safe-deposit boxes in London were still full. Eamon was to wait several years before transferring the balance of his wealth.

Once when admitting to the Governor of Jamaica, Sir John Huggins, that he had been in the munitions business during the war, Eamon whispered confidentially, 'It was a dirty business. I was glad to get out of it.'

He and Patsy were to die when their private plane crashed twenty years later. The local newspaper declared that 'The wealthy and popular O'Sheas would be sadly missed in Jamaican society.'

Prostitution

There are no successful games without
enthusiastic participants.

Leo Tolstoy

Books on anthropology make little mention of prostitution,
maintaining that primitive peoples practised polygamy from
an early age to conceal or obviate promiscuity. Sexual freedom varied according to custom and status, and attitudes of
society were readily adjusted to circumstances. In the
records of undiluted hypocrisy through the ages, the views
of men on 'loose women' must rank high in the charts. In
ancient times a middle-aged prostitute was a pariah, yet
those who condemned her nevertheless found it acceptable
for girls in their community to prostitute themselves to earn
their dowries, which would take between one and four years
depending on proficiency and aspiration. According to Dr
William Acton, who, in 1857, produced a learned paper on
the subject, any of those girls who subsequently chose to
make a career of 'granting sexual favours' were correctly
branded and treated as harlots. The same gentleman was
convinced that 'nice' women had no sexual feelings,
associating the act only with pleasing their husbands and
producing children.

Moral codes readily changed with religious attitudes to
penitents, brothel-keepers and finance. The early priests
encouraged young virgins to prostitute themselves for two
or three years before marriage to provide monies for the
temple coffers. Pope Innocent III refused to commit himself
on the subject other than to pronounce it praiseworthy for a
man not to marry a prostitute. The Ecclesiastical Courts of
the seventeenth century divided such women into three
separate classes: those kept by respectable gentlemen, those
who were self-employed for personal gain, and those who
lived in brothels. There is no record of how they were to be
judged but it was a practice in the eighteenth century for

directories to be published for the 'benefit and scrutiny' of gentlemen. In *Rangers Impartial List of Prostitutes*, published in 1775, the following description appeared: 'She has these many years kept the most celebrated Temple for performing the sacred Cyprian rites. Having amply sufficient for her immediate needs she is now concerned with providing adequately for her old age.' In his contribution to *Behind the Frontiers of Respectability*, published in about 1860, a worthy bishop, referring to attitudes to such women, stated that they were not to be confused with high-priced courtesans or fashionable society ladies who accommodated the Prince of Wales.

Contrary to popular belief, there are very few prostitutes who make a great deal of money for any period of time. Cross-examined in a New York court in 1983, a brothel owner declared that a competent prostitute 'with no shame' could earn as much as $2,000 a week but seventy-five per cent of this went to the management. He claimed that his success was achieved by his reputation for having no girls over the age of twenty-five: 'After that, they're on the street.'

The Prostitutes' Charter, produced in 1959, followed the passing of the Street Offences Act designed to remove prostitutes from the streets. Theresa O'Rourke, a most articulate hooker, speaking for the sisterhood complained, 'When I think what some of us have done for politicians, I no longer have faith in reciprocating goodwill. People do not take into account that, unlike any other business, we are not permitted to set off items like rent, lighting, heating and commissions against tax. There is no goodwill in our business and little opportunity to provide reserves for when the game gets overcrowded or we get beyond it.'

Appearing in a television programme subsequently, a very well-spoken lady classified herself as a 'specialist in the field' who only 'sold illusions' once a week. This enabled her to shop at Harrods, holiday in Portugal and pay her sons' public school fees. 'It was the prohibitive fees that set me off,' she added.

Some women are driven to the streets by sheer economic necessity; young girls are frequently attracted by being able to earn in a few hours what might otherwise take them a month, and some women find it an exciting and profitable hobby. The vast majority start off with the idea that it is only a temporary aberration. It is interesting that every major research into the subject of prostitution makes constant reference to the practitioners being driven to drink, criminality and destitution at relatively young ages. Except for the pimps and brothel-keepers, there is little, if any, mention of worthwhile or long-term financial rewards. Perhaps the only recorded exception is the 'Sex Nest' operated by Louis XV in the grounds of the Palace of Versailles. Poor members of the aristocracy encouraged their pretty daughters to pander to the king in return for which he guaranteed to secure them good marriages and dowries up to £20,000. In today's terms that would be equivalent to about £1,000,000.

The question remains whether it would be healthier for society and more profitable for the prostitutes if they were legally acknowledged as part of the service industry. In a more rational society it might be argued that the contribution made by some in obtaining international political favours, intelligence information and large export orders is worthy of financial recognition. As it is, the oldest profession in the world has the worst reputation, the least security and the poorest fee structure for those with the longest experience.

Mafia

A family is but too often a commonwealth of
malignants.

Alexander Pope

In 1969, the writer Mario Puzo hit the bestseller list with his
book, *The Godfather.* It stayed in the top ten for months,
sold twenty million copies and subsequently made one of
the most successful films of the decade. This was the book
that did more than any other to introduce the man in the
street to the family life, to the loyalties, the intrigues, the
strength and the horrors of those who control the Cosa
Nostra ('Our Thing'). Power is the name of the game, family
ties the secret of its success, fidelity the watchword, and
violence the accepted means of negotiation. The network of
the Sicilian underworld, which spreads from Europe to
America, has grown to control men and money, beyond the
worst nightmares of those entrusted with the welfare of
society.

Even honest, decent Sicilians, they say, are born with the
rules of the Mafia in their water and a clear understanding of
the difference between their brands of hoods and those of
other nations. They may well think of it as a select society, a
club of exclusive families, or a group of criminals, but the
description offered by an American Chief of Police is probably more accurate when he referred to it as a social disease.

The general view is that the Mafia, as it is now constructed, dates back to about 1860 although its principles
had long been a well-known part of Sicilian crime philosophy. In his book, *La Sicilia e La Mafia*, Cesare Bruno gives
the following description of the 'genuine' Mafioso: 'He
dresses unpretentiously, respects everybody, is humble in
manner, keeps his temper under control even when abused,
and will always appear to forgive. He strikes death-blows
suddenly, having taken every precaution to go unpunished.'

The Capo, 'Head', a top brass, is always ready to serve his

fellow man and build up a bank of creditors. Nothing is ever
too much trouble when his connection or muscle is sought.
Men 'owe him', and many die in his debt. But if called upon
to pay, they pay. That is the System. That is part of *Omerta*,
the code of allegiance to the 'Brotherhood', to the Godfather and his family.

As long ago as 1901, the Mafia wielded power in New
York which made a mockery of the law courts and horrified
those without Sicilian blood in their veins. A typical case in
that year concerned two influential members of this exclusive society who were sentenced to thirty years' imprison-
ment for cold-blooded murder. The evidence was so fright-
ening and sensational that many could not understand how
they escaped the chair, but the accused, Palizzola and
Fontana, appeared unperturbed by the open-and-shut case.
They and their lawyers knew that they enjoyed the protection of those who 'owed them', and they appealed successfully for a retrial. At the second trial, with the same lawyers
and different judges, half the prosecution witnesses were
missing, due to sudden death or emigration. The men were
acquitted on grounds of insufficient evidence, and jubilantly
decided to celebrate with their families in the old country.
The city of Palermo declared a national holiday to enable the
inhabitants to line the streets and give an appropriate
welcome to the heroes. The civic procession in honour of
the Madonna was postponed so that the two rescued men
could be present when prayers of thanksgiving were given.

The Mafia continued to flourish, fear or money inhibiting
the efficiency of the authorities, and attacks of sudden blindness making many members of the police poor witnesses.
Politicians were quick to recognize the potential of a powerful electoral machine, and bribery, death and corruption
became big business. And thus the disciples of the Devil
bought privilege, standing and fame; and the quality of life,
as it had been known, became diluted.

For years, the Dons and the Capos were way ahead of the
law and those who tried to uphold it. In special situations,
assassins like Vincenzo Rimi planned their own imprison-
ment for protection or to establish foolproof alibis. For
relatively little money they were able to conduct their

normal businesses from well-furnished cells where they frequently orchestrated the elimination of their enemies. Mafia gentry, like Gaspare Pisciotta and Turi Giuliano who had allegedly betrayed or double-crossed their colleagues, were said to have been executed by remote control. Police recognized the hand of Rimi in their deaths but, as they had to admit, he was behind bars at the time. The coffins of Turi and Gaspare were hidden by magnificent wreaths, but no one was ever charged with their murders and their families remained silent. Vincenzo Rimi maintained his office in the State Penitentiary for twelve months.

Persuaded to explain the philosophy behind the Order, a Mafia leader, Willie Moretta, told his interlocuters that the word *traditore* as used by his peers inspired the fear of a sentence of death from which there is no escape or appeal. Nearly two thousand years ago this was the stigma attached to the early Christians who surrendered the Scriptures to the Romans. Today it is associated only with the Cosa Nostra which still contaminates major cities like New York and Chicago.

It is interesting that in the film of *The Godfather*, the barber-shop murder of the club owner, Moe Green, was based on the real-life execution of Albert Anastasia in 1959. There was nothing wrong with Albert except that his cohorts stopped trusting him. That is the point when track records, family connections and references are no longer practical or sentimental considerations.

Professional hit-men like Tommie Viola, known by the New York police as the 'High Executioner', came into their own at these times. Tommie himself eventually received a life sentence, and there was little that could be done to help him. In the case of his colleague, Jimmy Salamone, however, friends saved him by squealing to the Internal Revenue authorities that Jimmy had violated the income tax laws. Somehow, this case managed to take priority and Jimmy got away with six years. Likewise, in the case of Peter Licavali, charges for hijacking, murder, protection racketeering and gun-running took second place to tax evasion. When Peter had his jail-release party it was estimated that the cost would have paid the annual salaries of all the judges in New York. 'The Licavali family know how to celebrate!' exclaimed a member of the unholy dynasty.

Some may question the size of the money motive behind the organization. Precise figures are obviously not available but some pretty shrewd estimates have been made by those close to the facts. To appreciate the scope of the operations it has been maintained that organized crime in America alone nets around $40,000,000,000 a year. That is more than the combined annual profits of IBM, General Electric, United States Steel, Ford and a dozen other major US corporations. The American Mafia have an interest in a substantial part of this industry and are a major influence on the rest of it. Even the Tax Commissioner, Sheldon Cohen, expressed the view that known rackets alone could justify assessments, which could be upheld, in excess of $200,000,000. The laundering side of the Mafia billions provides permanent employment for straight and bent experts specializing in legalizing vast sums of money. Swiss banking secrecy stops here: unlike Central American and Moroccan banks, the Swiss do not provide their numbered accounts to known criminals. In more recent times the Catholic world was horrified to learn that the Institute for Religious Works, otherwise known as the Vatican Bank, had been a major laundry for the Cosa Nostra. To the distress of many, the allegations have never been challenged but several directors of the bank have resigned, one to be found hanging under London Bridge.

In a powerful, well-organized secret society where the Mafia Disease is a pseudonym for garrotting, inside information is difficult to come by. But every once in a while somebody sings. Someone known to be a respected member of the fraternity manages to negotiate a deal with the authorities and pays a ransom of information in order to escape the electric chair. Perhaps the best known in this category is Joe Valachi, whose revelations Robert Kennedy described as the biggest single intelligence breakthrough in combating organized crime. Joe wrote his 300,000-word autobiography for the American government, disclosing the power behind the Cosa Nostra, and the terror-filled lives of all those associated with it. Several of those fingered by Valachi enjoyed large, flower-wreathed funerals just before they were due to be arrested. Undertakers, florists and hit-men worked overtime coping with the sudden increase in business. Once Valachi started singing there was no stopping him, and every chorus produced new facts and figures related to such doyens of the Society as Zangarra, Luciano, Tony Bender and members of the infamous Mengani family. Another was Al Aquioci. When the police picked him up, his friends were convinced that he would join the Valachi Choir, and he was advised to stay in jail and enjoy its protection. Al was not looking for guidance, and made himself ill raising $100,000 bail. A week after he emerged from his cell, his friends put him out of his misery by slicing up his live body before setting it alight with petrol. Al had never opened his mouth to the police, but his death served as a warning to potential squealers.

Cross-examined about his 'legitimate' business, Valachi declared that he was in a specialized field of banking. 'If a man needs $10,000, I lend it to him less 20 per cent commission. That means that he actually receives $8,000 and pays me $2,000 a week for six weeks.'

'Have you any idea of the interest rate you were charging?' enquired his interrogator incredulously.

'I made no precise calculations. I reckoned that by my standards it gave me a satisfactory rate of return on capital. I didn't need an accountant to tell me.'

'What happened to people who couldn't pay?'

'They were encouraged to reconsider their position.'

It was estimated that Valachi had enough money on the street in this one financial exercise to give him around $200,000 a week. Another, a pin-ball machine saloon, produced $1,000,000 a year, and he had not even paid for the machines. This little saga began with 'offering' the owner protection at a nominal cost of $400 a week — the precise profit which one of the fifty machines produced. Within a year it had risen to $10,000 a week and then, one evening, the owner was invited to a dinner party. It was a convivial affair, and when the brandy and coffee arrived, Valachi said, 'My friend, you have been a good partner but I think your children would now like you to be a manager.'

Learning that even the police could not guarantee to protect his family, the man accepted $100,000 for his business and moved to a quiet life in Delray Beach in Florida.

'That's the type of deal I understand,' Valachi wrote in his autobiography.

That document earned him the right to live in a small cell in solitary confinement for the rest of his life. He had no visitors and he made no demands. In turn, he was allowed to choose his own time for his daily exercise and was always accompanied by two armed guards. Part of their responsibility was to taste his meals before he did. Valachi was convinced that the Cosa Nostra would get him in the end. He was wrong — he died of cancer.

Another songster was Tommaso Busetta, a Mafia chieftain, who, in 1985, suddenly decided that allegiance to the Mafia code of honour, the *Omerta*, had been overstretched when his brother, two nephews and a son-in-law were murdered by the Corleonesi clan. He sang so loud that the Italian police were able to arrest some three hundred and fifty of his erstwhile colleagues. When the parties were formally charged they all appeared in the specially constructed court in individual cages. With over three hundred lawyers involved, it is estimated that the trial could well take a year. Even with bosses like Luciano Liggio among the captured, it is already known that more than a hundred of the leading Mafia drug traffickers escaped the police net. Even so, it is still the best and most unexpected haul ever to be made.

During the last twenty-five years the publicity given to the Mafia and the numerous books published about it have enlightened many, but have done little to limit its role in the world of crime. Edward Allen in his book, *Merchants of Menace*, refers to the 'international organization trading in violence, robbery, narcotics, gambling, kidnapping and labour racketeering'. He writes of hate, fear and intrigue, and underlying it all is the anxiety that there are still too few people in high places who are making sufficient effort to eradicate the blight from our society.

In 1976, A. Yards produced a study, *The Mafia Syndicate* which he dedicated to the memories of John and Robert Kennedy. His final conclusion was that, so long as the Mafia exists, American society remains in jeopardy. Most people believe that a $40,000,000,000-business simply isn't going to disappear in a hurry.

THE MONEY JUNGLE

You can fool all the people all the time if the
advertising is right and the budget is big
enough.

Joseph E. Levene

It might well be said that the world of finance is full of open
doors and closed minds. A cosmos for those who seek
wealth, power, influence, and the pleasures and excitements
that can be bought with them, it is a universe uninhabited by
poets, philosophers or prophets, and insulated by layers of
ambition and greed. It caters for those who confuse affluence with happiness, riches with security and prices with
values.

The world of finance is a grand circus where the tightrope
has no safety net. Where those who enter the arena crave to
manipulate the puppets and pander to the clowns. Where
the thrills of achievement are measured by the animals danc-
ing to the tunes of the cash registers. This is the globe for
marionettes to laugh away their years of fantasy until disillusionment sets in.

Within the real world, man has created this world of
finance to attract, organize, invest and mismanage the
monies generated by those who cannot accept that megalo-
mania is a terminal disease. For generations we have
become dependent on it, treating it with the respect and fear
ideally reserved for the Deity. If one considers the astronom-
ical wealth involved, it must be conceded that in terms of
real values, the world of finance is in debt to society.

Money Ethics and Practice

The secret of success is sincerity. If you can
fake that, you're made.

Anon.

Collins English dictionary defines the word ethic, from the
Greek *ethikos*, as a moral principle or set of moral values
held by an individual or a group. It forgets to mention that it
varies according to the codes acceptable in different societies at different times. Sacrificing moral principles has been
the practice of sovereigns and lesser mortals throughout
history. The Bible tells the story of King David, the great
poet, arranging for one of his loyal army officers to be killed
in order that he could take over his wife. Yet the king is
remembered for his psalms. This might rightly be considered a rare example but, women apart, there is nothing like
money to help a man come to terms with a bad conscience.
In the eighteenth century, a certain Mathew Dugdale insisted
on reciting prayers to his slaves each morning. The fact that
these chained wretches had been purchased, body and soul,
for £100 each, did not conflict with his moral principles.

Ever since the days when camel-traders exchanged
women for silk, theologians and teachers have besought
their disciples and their students to maintain high moral
standards when indulging in commercial practice. And well
they might. For in the jungle of trade, the scrolls of history
record that honesty is a moving target, oil is thicker than
blood, and moralists rarely make the main board. Mark Twain,
the great essayist, once wrote that there are two kinds of
Christian morals — one is public and the other is business.

In reality, fiction, facts and statistics show that the vast
majority of business men are genuinely honest — until the
price gets too high. Long before the wealthy could be numbered in their thousands, Charles Oelrichs went on record as
saying that no man ever made a million dollars honestly.
Having repeated this numerous times in rich circles, he was

amazed that he was never once contradicted. Among the ranks of the cynics, there are many who believe that there is nothing like preaching ethics as a substitute for practising integrity. Chastising employees and children for pinching postage stamps and sweets builds a man a reputation among those who need or respect him. It also helps the man himself when, in the privacy of his study, he makes false declarations on his tax return. Maintaining the same moral rectitude, he will then submit an inflated claim to his insurance company. It is these self-induced bouts of schizophrenia that enable some men to sunbathe contentedly in Cannes while others languish wistfully in jail.

Recording a discussion on integrity with Winston Churchill, the newspaper mogul, Roy Thomson, recalled saying, 'Winston, it pays to be honest.' The Prime Minister's response was: 'Have you considered the possibility of other reasons?'

In a later chapter in this book, I refer to honesty in the insurance business. It is not quite in the same category as morals in a strip club but there are certain similarities. At least men who enter these establishments, however, have an idea of what they will get for their money: that cannot always be said of those who pay insurance premiums. The latter group may be faced with irrecoverable losses; the former can only lose their reputations.

Prior to his discharge, at the end of a long prison sentence, the notorious burglar, Sam Shockley, was questioned by the priest as to whether he now believed in honesty. 'I believe in it, Father,' Sam replied. 'I simply don't know if I can afford it.' He was probably being far more honest than he realized.

The pages that follow deal with different aspects of business and investment practice and philosophy. It would be less than correct to imply that only rogues, knaves and two-timers inhabit the jungle of commerce. It is not so. Even in a world where men are driven forward by necessity, greed, ambition and vanity, it is a good trait to trust everybody. Just be sure to get any business agreement in writing.

Accountants

Financial advisers can't help you take it with
you, but then that's not the place where it
comes in handy.

F. Allen

There are none with greater involvement in the financial
affairs of men and money than chartered accountants. Their
standing and areas of expertise often fail to be appreciated,
and the services they provide are frequently not understood.
The important fact of which one can be completely sure
about an accountant who is chartered is that he is qualified.
This ensures a level of commercial intelligence and financial
understanding for which, in that field, there is no higher
qualification. But in itself this does not guarantee financial
expertise in all areas, or flair in applying knowledge, or any
great negotiating ability. There is no syllabus that could
possibly cover these, and it is important that the limitations
are appreciated.

Like the GP, the average accountant is not a specialist and
therefore has distinct limitations in the areas of diagnosis
and treatment. In the more sophisticated areas of takeover
techniques, overseas tax and bankruptcy it is often essential
to appoint a practitioner who has made a special study of
the particular subject. This invariably takes you from the
small partnership to the larger firm.

When about to appoint a new accountant, the following
points should be considered very carefully:

1 Make up your mind why you need his services. Is it for
personal tax advice, auditing, financial planning, negotiating skills, business guidance, commercial planning, insurance advice, investment counselling, financial structures
overseas, long- or short-term family financial planning, or
for expertise peculiar to your particular business or
occupation?
2 Make sure that the accountant knows exactly why you

think you need him. It avoids misunderstandings.

3 Try to assess whether he is competent to advise in all such matters (insurance and investments, for example, are two highly specialized areas). You are seeking expertise, not simply the views of someone who understands the subjects marginally better than yourself. Remember, you are looking for a competent adviser and not a well-connected intermediary or a camouflaged agent. (Incidentally, should the accountant receive any commissions from agents or brokers when acting for you, he should disclose these, and at least a proportion should be credited to your account. Most accountants do have direct or indirect commission arrangements. They are not uncomfortable taking such kick-backs and are usually not too sensitive to share them. The branch offices of major firms invariably have strict guidelines to follow in such instances. The smaller partnerships create their own set of rules.)

4 It is essential that you should feel complete confidence in telling your accountant every single fact relating to the financial affairs of your family and yourself. Your wife's earned or unearned income must be disclosed in exactly the same way as your second home or your plans for early retirement.

In discussing your future, your business or your family, it is also important that your accountant should be aware of any concern which you may have regarding your state of health. There is little point in encouraging him to help you make long-term business projections or investments if your doctor does not share your optimism. If you do not feel completely confident in revealing data of this kind you have the wrong accountant. It does not matter whose fault it is, the fact remains that you are expecting him to perform without all the facts. Take a fresh look at him and either decide to trust him completely or change him.

5 Too many people tend to think of their accountants as financial gurus who should be able to read next year's Finance Act through crystal balls. In practice, their function is to be familiar with the fiscal laws and understand

how they should be applied. This necessitates keeping up
to date with the many changes in tax law which are introduced each year. Despite the important and often essential professional service provided by chartered accountants they are still not formally listed among the 'exclusive'
professions. This fact is probably long overdue for correc-
tion, but the position is hardly helped when major firms
like Price Waterhouse list 'integrity' among their virtues.
This is rather like the Church feeling a need to describe a
bishop as trustworthy.

6 A word of warning. When you make an appointment to
meet your new accountant, you are entitled to expect the
courtesy of his undivided attention. If he takes more than
two telephone calls during your first interview, think twice
about whether to take him on. Either the man is not
organized or he has already decided not to rate you
highly as a client.

The small, suburban accountant should be able to provide
a very satisfactory service for most private clients, and for a
fair percentage of medium-sized businesses. It is unlikely
that he will have sufficient expertise or experience to cope
with the requirements of a major corporation, or with the
intricate planning often needed by a very wealthy client with
an involved estate. This should not be interpreted to mean
that the smaller accountancy firm might be negligent. It is
simply that it is less likely to have sufficient work in all areas
to justify its retaining the kind of specialist staff employed by
larger firms. This really is where a firm like Coopers &
Lybrand, with its network of suburban offices, can score
heavily over the relatively small firm. Unlike so many of their
smaller, provincial competitors, all their branch offices have
direct access to the entire expertise of their head office.
Where specialized skills are required, therefore, the smaller
firm is simply not able to compete, except possibly on cost.
It is a sad reflection on the accountancy profession that the
fear of losing a client inhibits the small firm of accountants
from asking the advice of a larger one. The cynic might be
forgiven for questioning the thickness of the veneer that
covers the image of professionals who nurture such reserv-

ations and doubts. The entrepreneur, on the other hand, would recognize an opportunity for one of the larger firms to establish a professional advice bureau for the benefit of less well-informed colleagues. The potential must be considerable. A streamlined professional service would not be difficult to administer, with profits and benefits accruing to all. Maybe it is simply a question of integrity. In the meantime, the opportunity has not been missed by all, and a select number of specialists, like the international tax adviser, John Chown, provide an independent tax-consultancy service for banks, major corporations and members of the profession.

In practice, larger firms of accountants like Arthur Andersen, Deloitte's, and a handful of others, are certainly better placed than many to serve major clients. Their extensive libraries, their international network of intelligence and their large panel of in-house experts must invariably give them the edge over their smaller competitors. For, even assuming that they had the knowledge, there is no way that a five- or ten-partner firm could consistently produce the quality of publications which firms like Arthur Andersen & Co. continually issue for their clients. Such firms can afford departments of top people who do little else. A typical example of these publications is a small booklet on customs duties which clearly illustrates how substantial overheads can be saved by the introduction of careful planning. It is doubtful if most accountants have ever given the subject more thought than they do to a duty-free shop.

But in the area of innovation it is not just the top nine who have claims to fame. Some of these have taken a long time to arrive or, it might be said, have remained unchallenged too long. In the category below them are several firms who could well join the elite few in the next ten years. Some have built their reputations on specialization in growth or trouble areas such as computers, oil, liquidations and insurance. Others have succeeded in providing a business management service in the form of sophisticated financial consultancy. Stoy Hayward, the 800-strong UK partner of the large international network of Howarth and Howarth is probably one of the foremost success stories in the last twenty years. Concentrating on providing a partner-to-client personal service, this firm recognized that many potentially large clients do not do justice to a meeting because they are too worried that the fee-clock is ticking overtime. Stoys simply abolished fees to senior partners; their overheads instead being built into the overall costs of the firm. Unlike most of their largest competitors, they pride themselves on adopting an entrepreneurial approach to the problems of their clients. Proof of their success is illustrated by the fact that all their top public-company clients have consistently out-performed the *Financial Times* Index for years. Not content with being good financial advisers, they have specialized in becoming the financial arm of each client, and the post-graduate training which they give their senior staff lays considerable emphasis on this philosophy. The system has worked, and the firm grows larger every year. Few appear able to emulate the style or achieve the same success rate.

Regardless of the size of firms of chartered accountants or the technical expertise of its partners, it is a mistake always to believe that they are automatically the best negotiators in any given situation. Often they are not. It can frequently pay a client to present his own case to the inspector of taxes — he is not as remote as he is made out to be. After all, the client should understand the nuances of his business better than anyone else, and should be able to present his case better. Those who decide to take this route, however, ought first to check out their story with their accountant. He will not necessarily try to dissuade you, and indeed may encourage you. But he will want to be consulted beforehand — apart from its being a matter of courtesy, he is likely to be far better qualified to appreciate the tax implications and could well stop you putting both feet straight in. In any event, he will need to be kept informed of your direct negotiations with the inspector.

In the professional area, as in many others, the business of claims is a growth industry. It might be called the American Disease but it has caught on in England in a big way; fortunately, in this country, lawyers are not permitted to take a share of the proceeds so it is assumed that, by and large, counsel keep closer to the real facts and the bona-fide witnesses. Otherwise, the general attitude and philosophy to claims in this country is similar to that on the other side of the Atlantic — make the companies pay! It starts off on the basis of suing for compensation. This develops into damages for real losses, and then moves on to undetected losses, potential losses, projected losses, until eventually a special breed of accountant is brought in. His job is to check the arithmetic and give an independent assessment of damages. No matter how long it takes him, or what method he uses to make his calculations, the answer is always the same. Blood.

In recent years most of the largest firms of accountants have come unstuck from time to time with professional indemnity claims. They have been sued for millions of pounds and dollars on grounds of insufficient care and attention, more commonly known as negligence. Sometimes the accusations are quite unjustified, but often they are not. A typical case concerns the takeover of a company with a chequered past. A major bank instructed a large firm of chartered accountants to carry out an investigation. It was agreed that the purchase price of the company would be equal to six times the average annual profit of the previous five years. Eventually, the figure was fixed at £30,000,000 and the transaction was completed. Shortly afterwards it was discovered that by cancelling the consequential loss policy of the company, the previous owners had produced a saving of over a million pounds a year, thereby increasing the sale price of the company by £6,000,000. The case against the accountants was that they should have noticed this fact when carrying out their investigation. On the face of it there was no answer. But underwriters facing a six-million-pound claim reckoned it was worth a few thousand pounds to defend the case on the gospel of the outside chance. After all, optimism knows no boundaries, and there's always the remote possibility that the claimant will retain an inadequate or alcoholic counsel. But not in this case. Two firms of solicitors, three QCs, two juniors and nearly two years later, the insurers settled for some eight million pounds. Professional fees, expenses and interest made up the difference between this amount and the original claim. The bankers were among the smiling. Had they chosen a firm of accountants with inadequate insurance cover, their heads might have been on the chopper too. Choosing well-insured large firms of accountants to carry out investigations gives the bankers protection as well as experience for their money.

A case could certainly be made for a client to question the indemnity insurance carried by his accountants. Larger professional firms carry protection running in excess of £50,000,000, with premiums in seven figures. None the less, with the enormous pressures imposed by industry on the profession, they continue to be a source of anxiety to their insurers. This insurance overhead should also be borne in mind when considering firms that might be too large or important for particular work. An analysis of professional indemnity claims successfully made against the top nine firms in recent years would shock many of their clients. Whether or not any fair conclusions could be drawn is doubtful. It may be even more revealing to know how many of our major corporations have ever bothered to check the size of the insurance protection held by their accountants. Rather as with the aviation catastrophe, it is not the one big claim that is the financial headache. It is the *unheard-of* situation of four major claims in a year. Few firms are insured against this possibility. Is it time for an enterprising insurance broker to design a new policy for major companies — one which would top up the gap which might arise if accountants had too many claims in one year? A company like GEC may well decide to carry an extra £100,000,000 of cover, just in case. The possibility of a claim is not that remote: one only has to imagine the odd nought added to or excluded from some significant figures.

Finally, the accountant should be your financial adviser and confidant, competent to exploit every legal opportunity to minimize your tax liabilities without unduly antagonizing the Inland Revenue. At all times his first loyalty must be to his client, provided that he doesn't put his practising certificate at risk.

It is still surprising that the highly respected Institute of Chartered Accountants has not fought harder to have the profession controlled by statute. This would prevent any bookkeeper or clown describing himself as an accountant which, under present law, he can. Some of the following pages illustrate the importance of recognizing the different skills required by those who specialize in areas where too many qualified and unqualified accountants still tend to dabble.

Tax Planning and Tax Scheming

Income tax has made more liars out of men
than any number of women.

Amos Hargraves Jnr

A biblical commentator of the first century wrote extensively
on the economic practices of the early Patriarchs and their
illustrious descendants. In a determined effort to preserve
capital, it was customary to divide assets among as many
members of the family as possible. Subsequently, when tax
was imposed, there were those who were able to undervalue
their wealth in order to keep their tithes to a minimum. If
nothing else, the writings of the worthy scholar proved that
tax planning and scheming have some pretty early origins.

Over the years it has grown from a popular game for
dabbling amateurs into a highly sophisticated and profitable
business for innovative professionals. Long past are the days
when companies and affluent individuals were satisfied with
creaming off a little from the top of their profits. With the
imposition of high taxation (in England it reached 98 per
cent in the 1970s), tax planning became a science, and the
marketing of tax schemes grew into an industry in every
country where it was permitted to make profits. For many
years the poachers outwitted the gamekeepers as the latter
were often slow to recognize that the rules of the game had
been changed. With the introduction of confiscation taxes, a
new generation of financial hustlers emerged, who, enjoying
the discreet support of licensed advocates, created a new
pseudo-profession which rapidly collected a large clientele.
In the sixties and early seventies tax planners competed with
drug pushers in manufacturing illusions. The tax planners
made more money but, sadly, it was the drug-pushers who
survived.

By the time revenue authorities had recruited their own
innovators, several governments had lost countless millions
of pounds and dollars. Once the tax inspectors had tuned

into the avoidance techniques, they showed no mercy for the transgressors. Scheme after scheme was successfully attacked in the courts, and those who had paid fortunes for financial conjuring tricks were mostly deserted by their advisers to haemorrhage alone.

The line between tax avoidance — which usually follows legal means — and tax evasion can be a fine one. In practice, the most successful tax-avoidance programmes have been those skilfully structured as integral parts of good commercial practice. Those best equipped to weave a safe path through the minefields of tax legislation keep their secrets to themselves. One of the finest examples of the benefits derived from true professionalism is provided by the Vesty family. They enjoyed millions of pounds of benefits for sixty years before the Revenue perceived the legal loophole which they had been exploiting for six decades. No hole-in-the-wall exercise, it was simply taking advantage of the tax-avoidance opportunities available to those who were able to establish subsidiary companies in nil-tax territories. This was in the good old days when tax inspectors were not as astute as they are today.

Advisers on tax avoidance, frequently a euphemism for evasion, thrived mainly because of two reasons. High taxation encouraged many otherwise honest people to become devious in their thinking, and less pressure on their greed buttons was required to persuade people to adopt contrived schemes. When the revenue authorities on both sides of the Atlantic recognized the vast sums involved, they hit the tax-scheming market with a vengeance. The attitude adopted by the IRS in America was so tough that many of the accountants involved accepted that the halcyon days were over, and were obliged to resort to normal practice. Others still believed they could beat the system and continued to produce expensive schemes which could best be described as deferred litigation planning. Eventually, the IRS extracted their pound of flesh and, as happened so often, the tax plus the fees cost the client far more than he might have paid had he not taken advice.

In London, the Rossminster Group conceived somewhat involved, naive but legal plans to assist companies to avoid tax. These were mostly based on structuring non-commercial trading companies with artificial tax losses. Although, in principle, the scheme had all the right ingredients, it was not too difficult for Inland Revenue to prove that the schemes were over-contrived and lacked commercial credibility. Rossminster's enormous success was achieved by an inspired marketing programme successfully practised by the tax-wizard Godfrey Bradman. Instead of making use of advertisments and fringe agents, they simply offered accountants a third of their outrageous fees. They were not short of co-operation. Often armed with little more than a qualified opinion from an optimistic tax counsel, it was not difficult for accountants to convince their avaricious clients that Rossminster held the secret of legally avoiding substantial tax liabilities. The stereotype plan which would supposedly avoid, say, £500,000 tax on £1,000,000, required an up-front fee of not less than £60,000. The accountant who received £20,000 for his introduction soon found that a substantial part of his gross income was derived from Rossminster. For some years everyone lived in a world of euphoria. Rossminster prospered, tax counsel and accountants earned enormous fees from rubber-stamping the same scheme over and over again and the clients made whoopee in cloud-cuckoo-land. The festivities were not to last. Taking the law into their own hands, Inland Revenue raided the offices of Rossminster for details of clients, and immediately proceeded to issue tax assessments. There were no criminal charges whatsoever, it was simply a matter of disallowing the schemes and clawing back the tax plus interest. Millions of pounds of overdue tax were recovered, Rossminster went out of business, and Godfrey Bradman gave up tax planning and bought himself a public property company. The accountants held on to their fees.

In America, in the seventies, enterprising confidence tricksters joined the ever-increasing numbers of 'tax consultants'. Plans ranged from buying works of art at artificially inflated prices to grossly exaggerating the value of gifts to charities, both normally treated as tax-deductible. One particularly interesting scheme designed for a high-profit-making corporation, concerned a $30,000,000 medical research programme, the principle attraction being that the investment would be completely tax allowable and the profits ultimately earned would be tax free. A very impressive, 200-page brochure was beautifully produced, listing dozens of leading scientists, doctors and international authorities who had agreed to be associated with the research. Multimillion-dollar profits were forecast and many colourful pages of graphs and medical reports were produced to justify the confidence. It was not long before queues of professional advisers sought the opportunity to introduce gullible clients to the promoters. With the offer of a commission scale up to 10 per cent plus a profit-sharing arrangement, this was not surprising.

But for a shrewd British industrialist, all this money would have been subscribed and lost. He retained an unlikely investigator, an insurance broker who had an amazing record for getting at the guts of a proposition. Tracking down a cross-section of those allegedly involved in the research, the broker soon discovered that the entire exercise was an elaborate trick. Every single specialist named had been promised either a substantial fee or, alternatively, a substantial grant for some of the work to be carried out at a particular hospital. In turn, major hospitals and laboratories had been assured that vast grants would be forthcoming just as soon as the first stages of the research were completed. The promoters themselves were proposing to take initial fees of $15,000,000 and disburse a further $14,000,000 in fees and bribes. Of the balance, $250,000 was to be placed at the disposal of a small hospital in the West Indies for innocently acting as a post office for men of distinction and fictitious facts and figures. A large number of potential investors and their professional advisers retired with egg on their faces, and counted their blessings. The confidence tricksters left town before they could be prosecuted and the insurance broker received a fee of £5,000. It was believed that several similar 'tax plans' had already been launched, but wealthy scapegoats are not prone to advertise their mistakes to their shareholders. Many do not even change their accountants.

Time has proved that, whilst there are certainly exceptions, it is often far cheaper for Mr Average to pay his tax

than to allow himself to be inveigled into contrived tax-
avoidance situations. Those who contemplate diving into
these uncharted waters should remember that, as in casinos,
it is invariably the croupiers who make the money, not the
punters. Mediocre tax inspectors who previously occupied
senior government posts have long been replaced by some
of the best brains in their countries. Not only do these
people know their jobs, but they have until their retirement
to pursue suspicious cases.

In theory, the ideal combination for a successful tax
scheme is an experienced finance-act juggler, a wealthy
client and a gormless Revenue inspector. This is the Utopian
formula for a sophisticated variation of the three-card trick.
In practice, it doesn't work out like that. All too often, the
inspector has re-shuffled the pack, the client is allowed to
suffer litigation jitters for years, while the juggler increases
his bank balance. The moral is not to enter into any arrangement which appears:

1 Contrived.
2 Not readily identifiable with sound commercial practice.
3 Likely to take a long time to obtain Revenue approval.
4 To give your professional adviser or his agent a dis-
proportionately large fee regardless of whether his advice
is proved right or wrong.

Invariably, tax scheming is an operation designed to interest those who are worried about the profits they have
already made. Genuine tax planning is the art of arranging
financial affairs in advance to attract the minimum amount of
tax, and, contrary to popular belief, a good tax planner is
comfortable discussing his recommendations with the
Revenue, if he has to. A tax schemer uses his skill to stretch
his interpretation of the Finance Acts. He encourages the
hopeful, and prays that the tax gatherer will not challenge
his theories before his fees arrive.

In this jungle of confusion there are many with strong
doubts about tax schemers, or scorched fingers, who try to
practise do-it-yourself tax-mitigation ideas. At one end of this
long line of entrepreneurs are those who have gleaned their

expertise from neighbours and the Sunday Press and have convinced themselves that successful tax planning only requires a shrewd mind and a tame lawyer. At the other end are a much more optimistic bunch who make their decisions without regard for the law or professional guidance. One genius in the first category ended his thirty-year marriage in order to take advantage of a lower income-tax scale and the benefits related to Capital Gains Tax. In due course it was pointed out to him that, as the law stood then, he had pre-judiced his Capital Transfer Tax position and had also for-gotten the large income which would now revert to him from his ex-wife. Sheepishly, he suggested that they re-marry, but the good lady was not prepared to sacrifice her new-found freedom. Eventually she did, but she extracted a great deal more out of her husband than the Revenue would have cost him. This is one of the more amusing stories, and has two morals attached to it. The first is that only a fool attempts to be his own tax adviser, lawyer or brain surgeon. The second is to keep matrimonial considerations beyond the perimeter of tax considerations. Marriage can produce enough confusion without bringing it into competition with the Inland Revenue.

The other class of tax expert is the fiddler. He specializes in fabricating expenses, inventing insurance claims, restrict-ing most of his financial dealings to cash and moonlighting. There are no reliable statistics indicating what these folk cost the economy, but there is little doubt that moonlighting is a growth industry involving hundreds of thousands of people. There are those who discover its advantages through the misfortune of being unemployed, and others who feel emotionally qualified to treat it like a profession. For the benefit of the uninitiated, the sophisticated moonlighter endeavours to adopt the following life-style:

First, he registers at the unemployment exchange, usually declaring an occupation for which he is poorly qualified — a petrol pump attendant, for instance, might describe himself as a motor mechanic knowing full well that any potential employer will quickly see through him. He then studies the going rates for cash-paid part-time work like domestic clean-ing, odd-job gardening, private car washing, reserve nightwatchman or spare hand in a small store. For jobs such as these, the scale of pay is relatively high because the employ-ers have no other overheads and no commitments with such staff. The moonlighter only has to earn the equivalent of his old *net* wages to break even. This usually requires no more than three long days' work a week. After that, he is his own master and can decide whether to improve his financial position by working another day or two a week, or just to enjoy his new-found leisure.

His back to the TV camera, a moonlighter was once asked what satisfaction he got from avoiding a permanent job. 'I've got my golf handicap down to 12,' he answered promptly.

So long as mass unemployment remains a permanent feature of British life, moonlighting will attract an increasing number of those who have no alternative, those who find it preferable to poorly paid work, and a third class who enjoy the freedom it gives. If the total numbers involved were as few as a quarter of a million, they would be costing the tax-payer at least £500,000,000 every year. That is equivalent to the combined salaries of twenty generals, three hundred senior officers, two hundred sergeants and seven thousand privates. Then there would still be sufficient over to buy each one a two-week luxury holiday in the South of France.

It would also follow that if ever income tax again rose to the confiscation level of 98 per cent of the seventies, the thin dividing line between tax avoidance and tax evasion would again become difficult to discern. No doubt such a situation would once again produce more losers than winners, but regrettably some of the best brains in the country would again be employed to help to fight the system. This is no secret to the Inland Revenue, whose staff firmly believe that, as they plan new demands, there are those who are busy stockpiling tax schemes in readiness for the next battle of wits. This is the world in which chartered accountants, tax counsel, insurance companies and banks often flourish. The officers of some banks might feel hurt to be included in this select list but, as the majority of large tax schemes have depended on genuine or bogus loan arrangements, bankers have often been enthusiastic partners with those who professionally wage war against tax.

Banks and Bank Managers

If you would know the value of money, try to
borrow some from your bank when you need
it.

Benjamin Franklin

A wise cynic once declared that a rich man was only a poor
man with money. In the same vein, it would pay the majority
of people to realize that banks are simply moneylenders and
money marketeers with a self-made charisma. They have the
same moral standards as their forebears, the money-
changers of ancient times, who treated the temples like
exchanges. Today, their respectability and dignity is founded
on their size and on their assets. Only the innocent can
confuse them with benevolent institutions. The managers of
the banks, as in any other business, are trained to understand their trade, encouraged to patronize useful clients, and
paid to help customers make money for the banks.

In realistic terms, banks provide a multitude of financial
services, each of which should be checked carefully by those
seeking the best deal for themselves. Banks are in competition with each other for the business of the individual, and it
is up to the individual to ensure that he obtains the best
rates and the best terms available. It should never be
assumed that these will automatically be offered regardless
of the size of an account or the length of time it has been at
a particular branch. Not enough people appreciate that
banks make far more money from current accounts than
they do from their deposits. The latter earn money for the
clients, the former, when in credit, earn money only for the
banks.

In a competitive market, few people would buy all their
goods from one supplier. On the same premise, it follows
that it is prudent to have two bank accounts with different
banks. This enables one to compare services, interest rates
and efficiency, and tends to make managers adopt a less

independent attitude. There is absolutely nothing sacrosanct about banks except the image which they have of themselves. Contrary to popular belief, interest rates vary a great deal in the banking jungle. When borrowing money, the fees and interest rates of several banks should be compared. If possible, you should find out what rates are paid by employers, trade associations and affluent friends: there is a very good chance that your own bank will readily meet the lowest of your quotations. It is important to bear in mind that unless an individual is wealthy, or controls or influences a substantial account, his personal goodwill is worth very little to any bank; to overestimate its value, or to forget that the first loyalty of even the nicest bank manager is to his bank, would be foolhardy. This is not a criticism; it is simply a reminder to the naive that banks pay their staff to enlarge their clientele not their social circle.

It follows that there is absolutely no mileage in being emotional about a bank that is charging more than a competitor of equal standing. To appreciate this point it is worth examining the true value of a saving in interest rates. The following is a typical example:

Loan	Bank A Interest	Bank B Interest
£10,000	Base rate + 4 per cent	Base rate + 2 per cent

(Major banks tend to adopt identical base rates)

The difference of 2 per cent equals £200 in normal terms, but it is equivalent to £400 of earnings for a person taxed at 50 per cent and £800 for one taxed at 75 per cent. Even for someone in the lowest tax bracket, around £300 has to be earned to pay a bank interest of £200. This is always assuming, as in the vast majority of cases, that the interest is not allowable for tax relief. To see these figures in focus, consider how many people able to borrow £10,000 are happy to give £400 a year to charity. Yet there are many thousands who, without any pressure at all, make such contributions to the profits of their banks.

A reliable client who borrows is worth more to his bank than he who stays in the black. Unlike the clergyman who

negotiates with his Master for your credit rating in the Here-
after, your bank manager is dedicated to his employers to
make profits on earth — from your account. So check his
terms, compare his rates and do not be afraid to transfer
your account if you find him wanting. A new bank manager
often feels a greater incentive to please than one who
believes your departure will give him one little headache
less. His real anxiety is produced by his area manager, or his
head office which is continually expecting greater profits
from his branch.

Inflexibility and greed cost several major UK banks some
of their best customers when American competition broke
into the London market. Often, a difference of less than a
half per cent was sufficient for a multinational corporation to
renounce a fifty-year association with their bank. Such
companies make their money by being unemotional and
using their banks to help them increase their own profits.
More individuals should do the same.

In 1963 one of our great clearing banks threw a retirement party for its well-respected chairman. He had first
joined the bank at the age of seventeen and had worked his
way, without the benefit of nepotism, right through the
ranks to become No.1 in this vast organization and a man
well-respected in the banking world. In the process, he had
served on numerous committees, represented his country
on countless enquiries and earned the honour of a knight-
hood. A gifted speaker, a shrewd thinker and a remarkable
negotiator, he enjoyed the respect of his peers and the
regard of his adversaries. When challenged to declare the
main lesson he had learned during his forty-seven-year
career, he was expected to produce a trite comment on the
subject of success, friendship, opportunity, ambition, dedica-
tion or luck. Not at all. After hesitating for an unduly long
time he expressed the wish to be excused from answering.
Pressed to do so, he announced between gritted teeth, 'It is
good to remember that when the chips are down, it is every
man for himself.'

Not many years later, when the fringe-bank-property crisis
hit the City, the attitude of the directors of the bank under-
lined the accuracy of his statement. In a sanctimonious style

adopted for the occasion, they viciously attacked those who, through poor judgement and inadequate experience, had lost fortunes in the commercial areas in which they had no business to operate — for, because of these people's mismanagement, the clearing banks had been unable to recover some of their multimillion loans. It was all true, but the bank spokesman had forgotten to mention that it was the banks themselves that had granted these vast loans to those with limited knowledge and even less experience: there is no record of any fringe-banker or optimistic property-owner breaking into a bank to obtain his loan.

As might be expected, it was sheer greed that had encouraged both the banks and the speculators. The latter believed that property prices could only rise, while the former competed with each other to make advances on the expectations of the dreamers. A typical proposal would be presented in the following form:

Company A, already fully geared, agrees to buy a derelict site for £1,000,000. It employs a solicitor who specializes in haggling to defer exchange of contracts as long as possible. In the meantime, the company directors manage to obtain planning permission to erect a 50,000-square-foot office block. This is where the fun starts. Rough estimates of building costs produce a figure of £2,000,000, making the total cost, at that time, in the region of £3,500,000, including interest and fees. At an estimated rental of £10 a foot, it is not difficult to appreciate that the new property could well earn a rent of £500,000 a year. At this point the exercise is discussed with a pension fund, whose representatives confirm that, given half a chance, they would happily buy the property for fourteen years' purchase, namely £7,000,000. Their only condition is that the property should be let to one first-class tenant. In the dream world of property developers of the 1970s this presents no problem. So, armed with such a watertight investment, Company A presents the proposal to a clearing bank with a simple request for a 75 per cent advance — that is, 75 per cent of the ultimate sale price. How incredible it seems today that the bankers vied with each other for this business to the point where they were happy to offer 90 per cent.

These schemes worked like charms for a few years.
Fortunes were made by the property developers, and
bankers with tunnel vision revelled in their illusions. But
such times were too good to last. It was bordering on the
ridiculous to expect the speculators, completely inebriated
with their success, to question their luck. What is amazing
was that the great city bankers continued to live in cloud-
cuckoo-land right until the balloon went up. Those were the
days when there were more bank managers than chorus
girls being entertained for lunch at the Ritz and the Savoy.

In the event, the prices of land plummeted, the property
market became temporarily saturated and there were no
tenants to occupy the buildings. This prevented the pension
funds from buying, and stopped the banks from advancing
moneys against the building costs. The property boys had
invested or spent their money, while half-finished buildings
and derelict sites lost 60 per cent of their values. The party
was over. The property developers had no money to pay
outstanding interest and the banks were obliged to hide
their blushes behind some of the largest debts ever accumulated. It was against this background that the directors of
some of Britain's major banks blamed their losses on property speculators and gamblers. Such is the integrity of men
under pressure. Still, none of the main bankers were actually
found with their hands in the till; furthermore, none were
known to exploit the distressing situation to their own
advantage as did their colleagues across the Atlantic at the
time of the Great Crash.

Following the débâcle of the seventies, the banks licked
their wounds and did their best to rebuild an image of
conservative thinking and non-speculative lending. This was
achieved to a remarkable degree in almost record time. But
it was not to last. Within relatively few years, the banks were
again financing highly speculative projects. While they were
a little more wary about property, they became obsessed
with the age of computers and, again, forgot to temper
enthusiasm with caution. But we still live in the days of
miracles and banks survive, often despite themselves. (*See*
'Bank Games'.)

Gone are the days when banks were only concerned with

lending. Today they expand their profits by selling insurance, arranging and providing mortgages, and taking a major role in the fields of investment trusts and money management. They obviously have the largest captive clientele in the entire financial services arena. All they now need is to develop the expertise necessary to ensure that their customers are well advised. Until then, nervous bank managers will continue to lace their diets with tranquillizers and take early retirement when it is offered.

For those who still hanker after a personal service reminiscent of the times often referred to as normal, all is not lost. There are still a few long-established, highly reputable banks that provide an individual service for those prepared to pay a relatively modest extra to be treated as privileged clients. Such banks, which have long specialized in this exclusive area, carefully choose their employees with as much emphasis on character, personality, appearance and manners as on A Levels. They act for those who demand or need the confidential and objective attention which most of the larger banks are no longer able to give. Among the small number who operate in this exclusive area is Coutts & Co., the two-hundred-year-old family concern. They act for Royalty and some thousands of others who require something better than the post-office service which the majority of customers are obliged to accept. Banks like Coutts expand almost entirely by recommendation rather than by advertising, and they survive because of the unique service they provide.

Bank Games

Without hallucinations, a lot of big money
would remain uninvested.

H.L. Menken

Monopoly, the family game that for over fifty years has brought hours of fun to millions — and a fortune to those concerned with its invention and manufacture — is probably the most successful money game invented. It has also introduced to many the challenge, excitement and basic terms of property dealing. But, for the majority, the Bank in Monopoly is the nearest anyone could imagine the serious business of banking being associated with a game. Normally, there is nothing remotely amusing about providing loans, letters of credit, deposit facilities and other banking services. They might be described as useful, enterprising or simply dull, but amusing they are not.

There is, however, another side to banking which requires an enormous amount of ingenuity and humour to appreciate. This relates to the big money syndrome where banks join forces to provide jumbo-sized loans to governments. To over-simplify the exercise, the procedure progresses along the following pattern:

The government-owned Bank of Negado decides to finance a three-hundred-mile motorway costing $500,000,000. Their security is the Negadan government which, though known to be economically fragile, has not reneged on a loan for a long while. In no time at all, an organization such as Citibank in New York or Warburgs in London is approached to put together a consortium of banks prepared to grant a ten-year loan to Negado. With the banks flush with money waiting for a long-term home, and prevailing interest rates at around 9 per cent, a bond is produced for $500,000,000 at an interest rate of, say, 10 per cent. Around fifty to a hundred of the world's largest banks will subscribe, relieved that they can forget about part of their cash pile for ten years. The provisional agreement probably takes less time to arrange than the average private mortgage. The innocent onlooker might almost assume that the Bank of Negado had a queue of lenders waiting for the opportunity to lend it a mere $500,000,000. The directors of banks who have not been invited to participate are deeply offended and retire determined not to invite the promoters to join when they are structuring a loan to one of the Third World or Central American countries. In due course, half-page announcements appear in the *Wall Street Journal,* the *Financial Times,* and other papers, telling the public that the Bond is fully subscribed. In small print it is also mentioned that there's no room for private individuals or others who might have wished to participate. Thus, in one simple move, a loan equivalent to the entire funds of most of the participating banks is made to a government which has anything but a stable history. It is not even as if the loan were to be used to import American and British goods and thereby create a boom for manufacturers and a little hope for the unemployed. No, the money is for a motorway which will, it is hoped, be built by Negadans in Negado. (This is not meant as a criticism: deals of this kind fall into the normal pattern of international banking and are simply an extension of day-to-day activities among those who make borrowing and lending their business.) But this is just a prelude to the real game; the fun is yet to start.

The players are now in position, the moves can be anticipated by some, and it is only the timing that is uncertain. Negado has the money and holds all the trumps and, for the benefit of the uninitiated, there is no umpire and there are no fixed penalties for cheating. On the sidelines sit the cynics and the cowards who lack the enthusiasm or the courage to join the fun. At this stage there is no reason to believe that the investment is anything other than sound, providing a higher than average return for the lenders.

Motorways are not built overnight so, at the end of the first year or two, there is still plenty of capital left from which to pay the interest. This appears in all the balance sheets, no questions are asked, the bankers are relaxed and the good name of Negado is slightly enhanced.

Come the fourth year, the President of the Bank of Negado arranges to be invited to New York where he is fêted by the Mayor, the local Senator, the Chief of Police and the officers of all the major banks in the city. Five hundred guests have a gala evening at the expense of a city that cannot afford to repair the holes in its main streets. The following day, the Negadan pays a courtesy call on the US bank directors involved, to bring good news and bad news. The good news is that he has come personally to tell them that, while the interest on the loan cannot be met for the coming year, the proposed increase in taxes should enable his bank to catch up the following year. The bad news is that if the lenders attempt to sue the Bank of Negado the government will be compelled to place it into liquidation.

Coded telexes make the rounds of the lending partners, who unanimously agree that on no account can they afford to foreclose. The following day, the financial papers publish a statement that there are no problems with the Negadan loan. In the meantime, in accordance with the rules of the game, the consortium brings in a recycling expert. His function is to submit recommendations whereby, on paper, the Bank of Negado will immediately repay the loan in consideration of a fresh loan for another £500,000,000 plus the interest outstanding, making a total of £550,000,000. This satisfies the lenders' accountants, avoids any bloodletting in the banking world and upholds the good name of Negado. In recognition of the arrangement, the borrower agrees that future interest should be calculated at 10 per cent.

To date, no one has had the courage to calculate the aggregate value of recycled loans. All that is known for sure is that if any banking partner ever pulled out of the game, half the major banks in the world would go broke overnight.

The satirical writer, Art Buchwald, once wrote a column on this subject for the New York *Herald Tribune*. In it he considered the opportunities for the enterprising recycling agent who made contact with borrowers immediately any loan was agreed. At the least, such a character might save the cities of London, Zurich and New York the cost of all those expensive parties.

By any normal criteria, it is difficult to understand many

major decisions made in the international banking world. The simplest explanation may well be that the gurus are guided by the conviction that, in a nuclear age, money only has a limited life anyway.

Mystics and Croupiers

When the masses confuse mythology with
reality, the materialists always win.

J. Stanislaw

Betting shops provide fantasies of instant profit without the
anxieties created by long-term expectations. The world of
investment and unit trusts enables people to dream that in
this tax-ridden society there are some financial oracles
blessed with the gifts of prediction once reserved for the
prophets; and dedicated advertising agents successfully
convince the gullible public that these mystics have
extended their powers to the *Financial Times* Index on
behalf of a particular unit trust. In a limited number of cases
a trust's spectacular performance might well justify the
eulogies. It is true to say, for instance, that anyone who
made an initial investment in, let us say, M & G or Perpetual
Growth would today be rich. Furthermore, like the US fund
managers, Tweedy Browne, these two growth funds seem to
have developed investment philosophies that have consistently out-performed the market by wide margins. The lucky
investors who placed their money in their trust can count
their blessings and their fortunes, but they are the exceptions among the exceptions.

Investment funds should reasonably be judged over a
period of not less than five years, and preferably longer. In
the seventies, a cross-section of twenty-five of the top unit
trusts managed to achieve an average annual growth of
minus one per cent over a five-year period. This allowed for
those which made losses of 10 per cent per annum and just
one which made a profit of 8 per cent. In practical terms,
investors would have been considerably better off leaving
their money in a building society or even on deposit in a
bank.

'Size,' screamed the fund managers, claiming that real money can be made only when one deals in large shareholdings and substantial sums. It is difficult to interpret the terminology when those twenty-five funds alone were already dealing in aggregate sums of £300,000,000. In a similar period those unenterprising investors who acquired dreary old National Savings Certificates made a tax-free profit of 37.9 per cent against a loss of 24 per cent suffered by holders of a basket of reputable investment trust units.

In the middle eighties there are certainly a reasonable number of fund managers who can boast some good profit figures, but financial gurus and clairvoyants do not abound in the industry. There are a fair number of 'better-than-the-index' performers but most of the outstanding track records are produced by those who manage private portfolios. Such fund managers, not accountable to institutions, can indulge their own fancies without the pressures that in-house competition and job-security anxieties invariably create. Those who doubt these conclusions might do well to analyse the performance of one hundred and fifty major investment trusts for the five-year period ending 31 December 1985. These funds managed over £1,500,000,000 and, on average, failed to keep pace with the *Financial Times* 30-Share Index. In the majority of cases, an investor who bought the Index was likely to make 20 per cent more than if he had been holding a basket of investment trust units. On the other hand, he would have trebled his money with M & G, Perpetual and just a few others.

On balance it might be said that advertising agents have done far more for unit and investment trusts than most fund managers have done for their clients. This is by no means a new phenomenon — as long ago as 1935 one of the largest managed funds in the United States saw their share price slump from $75 to 75 cents. This group had also boasted some of the best-qualified and highest-paid consultants in the land.

Over the ten-year period to the end of 1985 there has been a number of investment funds— like Confederation Life or Scottish Widows — who might well, along with those already mentioned, be considered star performers, having quadrupled investments entrusted to them. For cautious people looking for performance and security, they are certainly worth including in any carefully chosen portfolio of well-managed funds. The fact remains that advertisements can easily confuse, and, when buying, it is safest to invest with those firms with proven track records over periods of not less than ten years. It is a good idea to pay particular attention to performances when the *FT* Indices are down – fund managers that can predict this trend well in advance are often worth following. In 1974, the year when the Dow Jones dropped 34 per cent, for example, Tweedy Browne still managed a profit of nearly 2 per cent. That means that they beat the index by 36 per cent. Above all, never listen to excuses for poor management. Fund managers belong to the brotherhood of the highly paid – if they do not antici-pate a recession, do not blame the recession for your losses.

Those who prefer to be guided, on a weekly basis, in building their own share portfolio for capital gains are unlikely to make fortunes by listening to stockbrokers or subscribing to tip-sheets. Over many years recommend-ations made by 'Bearbull' of the *Investors' Chronicle* have out-performed the market by a very substantial margin. His articles make interesting reading, and his performance is consistently most impressive – in the eighteen months to December 1985 he achieved a capital gain of over 50 per cent. Anyone contemplating a DIY investment portfolio would do well to pay attention to 'Bearbull'.

Gnomeland

To preserve a secret, wrap it up in an enigma.
Giorgio Getcelli

Switzerland! Watches? Chocolates? Winter sports? No ports, no ships, no coal, no oil, no allies, no hydrogen bombs, no commonwealth, no alcohol, no member of the EEC, no casinos, no visible means of support. Its claim to fame is having stayed out of wars, political intrigues and international obligations for centuries. A small, unencumbered state closeted between Germany, France and Italy, it is insulated by its determination to remain committed to self-preservation within its own limited borders — a national policy which could be expected to breed enemies, to discourage the co-operation of neighbouring states and to inhibit progress. All the ingredients to be the most impoverished and unpopular nation in the continent of Europe. And so it might have been but for one unique commodity which only the Swiss have been able to sell with the piety normally reserved for priests. They market integrity.

Perhaps shrewder than the Germans and more conservative than the English, they may be less hospitable than the Italians and less glamorous than the French — but they do not pretend to compete in these areas. They do not attempt to camouflage business arrangements by heavy entertaining or confuse their clients with complicated agreements. Their success lies in their ability consistently to project an image of unquestionable credibility and to live up to it.

A history of poverty has made the Swiss money-conscious and careful. Memories are long in the Alpine villages where wages were low for generations and work-shy members of the community were unknown. Although people speak glibly of the 'average' Swiss, he is not easy to define as a type — in Zurich he is more like the German, in Geneva like the French, and in Lugano like the Italian. But as a tribe they have a great deal in common:

They are hard-working.

They are intrinsically honest.

They respect money to a point of worship.

They are modest, compared with all their neighbours.

They are tougher on criminals than most European countries.

They are determined to remain independent, regardless of cost.

While their reputation for keeping Switzerland for the Swiss was somewhat belied when they quietly provided refuge to many German refugees and war victims, it is true that they believe in keeping unemployment to a minimum at the risk of appearing distinctly inhospitable to immigrants. They do not argue with the criticism levied at them for 'importing and exporting' foreign labour to meet their industrial demands and to help balance their books. They are not concerned with solving the employment problems of the Italians and the Turks but they do use their labour when it suits them. It is part of a system they are not prepared to change because it works well for them.

Few of those who arrive in Zurich and Geneva carrying their fortunes are interested in the local domestic problems. Swiss secrecy, honesty and caution have encouraged thousands to deposit their surplus funds in the hundreds of banks that trade in that country. Most of this money simply lies there for years accruing interest for a rainy day. It is sacrosanct — so much so that countless numbers have died without their secret accounts being disclosed to anyone. This has, of course, produced gigantic profits for the banks which often hold these funds on current accounts, believing correctly that they will never be claimed. Swiss bankers may not be the most entrepreneurial investment managers, but this at least means that they do not speculate with clients' funds. They are masters of the art of earning with no risk: fortunes, in their care, may not grow — except for the interest they earn — but at least they remain intact.

The Swiss are not remotely concerned with the fluctuating popularity of foreign tycoons and politicians and those unable to trust the stability of the tax systems of their governments. In providing a money sanctuary they do not intentionally attract or accept money emanating from the Mafia or other bent sources. They may well be in the business of hiding money, but protecting the criminal and his ill-gotten gains is not part of their service. To understand the system it should be appreciated that Switzerland is a law-abiding, civilized and democratic country — it simply does not treat tax evasion as a crime.

There are those who, out of jealousy or conviction, question the moral standards of the bankers of Gnomeland. On balance, they are a tiny minority who are unable to recognize the benefits to be derived from having a major money centre where discretion and secrecy are the hallmarks of the operation. There is no other country in the world where the service agreements signed by bank employees come under the Official Secrets Act.

It is this remarkable reputation for integrity that has led numerous international industrialists to entrust their trade secrets to Swiss professional firms, who benefit substantially from the image created by their country. This is an area which requires an expertise which, in many countries, is often not readily available from accountants and lawyers. No doubt this is the reason why a number of relatively small firms like Curator AG in Zurich, Mandataria AG in Lausanne and Visura AG in Solothurn have built such prestigious clienteles. These companies specialize in providing legal, accountancy and tax services for those requiring professional expertise across national borders. An acknowledged expert in this field, Dr Hanspeter Hostettler of Curator, frequently finds himself on both sides of the Atlantic quietly advising corporations involved in the intricacies of international finance. It is in this world, where publicity is scorned, that the Swiss specialist excels both as a confidant and a professional.

It is almost impossible, nevertheless, to quantify the influence exerted by the Gnomes of Zurich. They rarely figure as corporate entrepreneurs, financial manipulators or innovators in the marketplace. Unlike Britain and America, Switzerland hardly goes in for merchant banking; wherever possible, the Swiss avoid the risk business, content to make their profits from careful investments in non-speculative securities. There are very few Swiss members of Lloyd's, and yet Switzerland has one of the largest and most respected re-insurance companies in the world. The Swiss neither compete with, nor offer the scope of, London or New York as money centres, yet, as strictly low-key operators, they might structure a vast loan to the World Bank, encourage an international consortium of bankers to support the American dollar or, with double security, re-finance a major national industry. They have a strange kind of modesty which enables them to move comfortably in an honest grey area, where their power is well-recognized but not advertised in any way: the President of the bank travels to work on the same tram as his telephonist. There is no need for Swiss bankers to announce that they can rustle up more money in less time than most. Everyone knows. That is their power. Treating confidentiality like a precious commodity and careful housekeeping like a creed, they manage to retain a kind of sanity in the world money market, a sanity unlikely to be found in London or New York.

The real mystery of the Swiss is why, with so much going for them, they smile so little.

PLAYING THE MARKET

Making Real Money

We must believe in luck. How else can we
explain the success of those we don't like?
Jean Cocteau

Facts and statistics confirm that, in every age, the vast majority of tycoons have made and continue to make their
fortunes from their own businesses. Not for them the hat-pin
and the financial Press, or the gin-sipping gurus that haunt
the bars of every money marketplace. These are single-
minded men who enjoy the challenge of hard work. Henry
Ford built cars; Simon Marks built a vast chain-store; William
Butler, a tobacco empire; Zaharoff, an arms market; Rank,
Guggenheim, Gestetner, Carnegie, Hanson, Kalms, and
countless more, all became wealthy by sheer hard work
coupled with determination and flair. In addition, they stuck
to businesses they understood. Their beautiful homes, their
charity trusts and their millions all came from long hours of
concentrated effort. Individually, each epitomized the definition of success as being 99 per cent perspiration and 1 per
cent inspiration. None of them depended on luck. This is
invariably the real secret behind every major story of
achievement in business and commerce. Such men are not
to be found among the financial cowboys who manufacture
dreams of making instant fortunes only to bring nightmares

down upon themselves and upon others whose money they lose. They were not listed with the 'Princes of the Seventies' who lost millions for people who were conned into get-rich-quick schemes. Men who build worthwhile corporations are workers not punters.

But there are those who do not fancy hard work. They believe that they can invest their savings and, without effort or knowledge, double, treble or quadruple their money. They believe in the fable of the alchemist who discovered the magic formula to make gold from copper. They build illusions of making real money from stocks and shares in companies about which they know nothing. They happily invest their after-tax nest-eggs on the strength of tips from clerks, hairdressers or chauffeurs, who are allegedly working for someone in the know. Others consistently put their trust in stockbrokers who are little more than the parrots of gurus poring over their charts in the backrooms. Most would average far better if they kept clear of shares altogether and only invested in Government Bonds and Securities. Not the stuff of which fantasies are made, true, but such investments cast no shadows of distress. They can be cashed quickly, too. Too many people who boast about the £1,000 that doubled in months from some amazing share all too often forget to mention the £5,000 loss they suffered elsewhere.

Those who habitually play the stock market share visions with others who are addicted to the roulette wheel. The main difference is that the latter group often derive more fun out of losing. Beyond the obvious reasons, people do not make money from the stock market because:

1   Most private investors are completely ignorant of the real facts about the companies whose shares they are buying.
2   They tend to worry, which makes it difficult, if not impossible, for them to think objectively. Like book-makers who never bet, many of the most successful and able financial advisers never buy a share for themselves or their families. They are content with the fortunes they earn from commissions. A Zurich investment consultant personally handles $1,000,000,000 of investment monies

on which he earns a half-per cent per annum; he has never bought a single share on his own account.

3   Too many amateur investors are influenced by tips rather than facts. They are reluctant to believe that those who are really on the inside track rarely talk. Those that do talk have not only bought already, they are more than likely planning to sell.

4   They are usually impatient for their profits or, even worse, afraid to take a loss. The professional decides, usually in advance, how long he will keep a share or at what stage he will cut his losses.

5   They cannot understand that the average stock-broker can barely afford the time to answer a telephone call from a small client, let alone to give him advice. In 1985, a successful stockbroker in a substantial firm had to earn more than £1 a minute in order to pay his own salary and his share of the overheads. He simply could not afford the luxury of chatting to timid clients with modest portfolios.

The Crowd Always Loses was the theme behind the noted work that F.C. Kelly wrote in the 1930s. How right he has proved to be. In the 1970s, hundreds of thousands of small investors, with no capital worthy of the name, finally summoned up the courage to buy shares just as the market was reaching its peak. The professionals thanked God for the innocent who bought the shares they were unloading. People in this category, unlike those referred to in the next chapter, should not buy shares at all. If they want to invest money which they are unlikely to need in a hurry, they should:

1   Buy their full entitlement of National Savings Certificates.

2   Invest in a unit or investment trust but only one of those with a first-class ten-year profit record.

3   Never make allowances for investment managers who do not get it right. Their job is to make profits not excuses.

Nevertheless, there are determined small investors who

have made money, real money, from investing in the share
market. They have not usually been stockbrokers or people
advised by them. Exceptionally brilliant men like Charles
Clore, or J.P. Morgan before him, were able to recognize
undervalued assets better and quicker than most men in
their time. Having carried out their own investigations, they
would then instruct their stockbrokers to buy, the value of
these men lying in their knowledge of the market and their
ability to buy a large interest without seriously affecting the
share price. They usually did a good job, but it was Clore
and Morgan who had the genius and really understood the
market.

The following investment guide was produced, almost by
chance, by a British business man who was neither a stockbroker nor a fund manager. He was a logical man who
reluctantly accepted a challenge to produce a philosophy for
a share portfolio. He was obliged to accept only two conditions: that he would not consult a professional adviser in the
money market, and that he would limit the exercise to ten
shares. He, in turn, made it a condition that he would always
conform to at least four out of the following five criteria, but
he should have one long shot in which he was allowed to
invest 2 per cent of the portfolio:

1   The executive chairman or managing director of any
company in the portfolio had to have a substantial
personal shareholding.
2   The share price had to be less than 70 per cent of
the asset value excluding any item for goodwill (such as
long-term contracts, patents and established business
connections).
3   The share could not be among those in the *Financial Times* or Dow Jones Indices.
4   In the absence of special circumstances, the share
would need to have earned a well-covered dividend.
5   The top executive would need to be experienced in
that particular business, and, ideally, should have either
launched or rescued it. It would also be preferable for
him to be under the age of fifty-five, not because older
people are over the hill but simply to make sure that he

won't be during the time the shares are being held.

6   The share price had to be well covered by assets, or there had to be very convincing reasons why this was not the case.

7   Finally, it was agreed that the portfolio would be held intact for five years, but any share that doubled, or fell by 20 per cent would be sold immediately.

The next set of rules were to apply after the shares had been acquired:

1   If the price rises by 50 per cent, sell — unless it is the subject of a takeover, in which case watch it and then take cash.

2   If the price drops by 20 per cent, sell. Do not look for excuses. It is not that sort of portfolio.

3   At the end of two years, give serious consideration to selling. This is intended as a 'performance' portfolio and, in the absence of special circumstances, look for another stock.

4   Never be in a hurry to buy. Never be afraid to sell and cut losses if necessary.

The business man took himself off to a reference library to analyse company reports and press comments that had appeared in the previous two years' issues of the *Financial Times*, *The Economist* and the *Investors Chronicle*. He obtained copies of the last annual reports from thirty companies and eventually chose the following: Racal Electronics, Trafalgar House, B. Mathews, British Land, Dixons, Lex Garages, Quinton Hazel, Land Securities, Hanson, and, the rank outsider, Hampton Goldmining Areas.

All these companies had dynamic chairmen — self-made men with large fortunes and, in most cases, substantial egos invested in their businesses. They were all full-time executives. At least six were under the age of fifty when the portfolio was put together in the mid-1970s. Hampton Goldmining Areas doubled soon after the purchase and was sold. (This turned out to be premature as the share eventually appreciated several hundred per cent.) The rest of the portfolio more than trebled in value within five years — a period during which the *Financial Times* Index rose by just 32 per cent.

The business man later admitted that, prior to producing this portfolio, he had been guilty of most of the faults listed earlier in this chapter. The philosophy has continued to work well for him and for others who followed it.

Of course, timing is important but, in theory, if a share meets the required criteria, the time should be right. Finally, the most important advice of all — if in doubt, don't buy. Remain liquid.

When one of the really successful US investment managers was asked the secrets of his success, he answered: 'I've never been afraid to sell and stay liquid. I firmly believe that buying opportunities are part of the market cycle. They are worth waiting for. My only other secret is to sell when I have a good profit. I never wait until I believe the share has reached the top — I'm happy to let the man who buys from me do that.'

No Loss Portfolio

What I know about money, I learned the hard
way — I had it and lost it.

M. Halsey

'Money makes money' is one of those worn-out clichés that
must have been hatched by an impecunious individual in
search of a reason for his financial insufficiency. It is a plati-
tude that conjures up a picture of two old tramps witnessing
directors of a large company pouring out of their offices into
their palatial cars. As they take alternate swigs from a label-
less meths bottle, one tramp says to the other, 'Has it ever
occurred to you that money always goes to the wrong
people?'

Unfortunately, there are others who are not meths drink-
ers, who have secure jobs and nice homes, who also believe
the adage. In truth, people make money. Money does very
little by itself. Most people who unexpectedly come into
money mismanage it and get their sums wrong in their
determination to show their friends and themselves exactly
how easy it is to make money make money. The fact remains
that most pool winners lose half their fortunes within two
years of celebrating their good luck. Those of modest
circumstances who inherit wealth usually take even less
time. As opposed to those referred to in the previous chapter, this class of person actually has capital to invest.

The problem is that too many people believe that all one
needs to double a fortune is a sharp pin, the *Financial
Times* and an unbiased financial genius. The latter usually
turns up in the form of a barber, a barman or an inveterate
loser. The consistency with which this happens defies the
law of averages and explains why so many large financial
windfalls bring disillusionment to the naive and the inexperienced.

Many people are able to cope with unexpected capital
two or three times their gross income. The £25,000-a-year

man, confronted with a new bank balance of £50,000 might well decide to extend his house, fill up the family with National Savings Certificates and spread the rest across a special holiday and a couple of well-chosen unit trusts. Somehow, though, when faced with £100,000, reason deserts him and his desire for security is eroded by a compelling urge to become an investment tycoon. This is the point when his brain-cells crunch their gears and sanity makes room for schizophrenia. A man who has been perfectly normal for, say, fifty years, is suddenly torn between dreams of security and fantasies of fortune. In his frenzied efforts to achieve both he succeeds with neither.

In practice, it is possible to safeguard the medium-term value of capital and simultaneously adopt a more adventurous attitude to building an investment portfolio. For this purpose it is assumed that £100,000 is available, after doing all the things one would like to do to celebrate or share one's good fortune. Those likely to be affected, apart from pools winners, are people who inherit, those who benefit from the cash values of substantial pension schemes, and an increasing number who are dumbfounded by the appreciation in the share options granted by their employers — a benefit which is likely to bring substantial sums to many thousands of employees in the future.

A practical compromise in producing a balanced investment programme is to ensure that, beyond all reasonable doubt, the capital sum will be available when it is likely to be needed. Furthermore, that a reasonable percentage would be readily realizable at very short notice, without loss. On this basis, 70 per cent of the capital could be so structured as to guarantee a substantial amount of liquidity and at the same time produce realistic capital appreciation. This would be achieved by implementing the following programme:

1   Invest £30,000 in the Warren Gilt Plan. This investment, guaranteed by one of the largest UK insurance companies and by the British government will produce about £75,000 at the end of ten years. That is assuming that the bonuses attached to with-profit endowment policies do not suddenly become taxable.

2   Purchase £10,000 worth of National Savings Certificates for your family and yourself. Maturity values, allowing for re-investment after five years, should produce around £20,000.

3   Invest £30,000 in a portfolio of low-yielding government stocks guaranteed to produce £45,000 tax-free in ten years.

This portfolio will produce the following benefits:

1   All the capital invested is 100 per cent secure.

2   Of the £70,000 involved, £40,000 is always available.

3   The investments will together produce a capital sum of not less than £145,000 in ten years.

4   It still leaves £30,000 — 30 per cent of the original capital — available for more adventurous ideas.

At this point the investor should consider the degree of risk that he wishes to accept. Of course, he could elect to indulge in playing roulette or backing horses, confident that his original fund is securely invested, but this is not the purpose of the exercise. Given a reasonable amount of time and intelligence, thought should be given to the investment set of rules set out in the previous chapter. The potential for real capital appreciation has proved to be considerable and the downside risk very modest indeed. Short of a slump or a vindictive government, one should be able to put together a share portfolio that will at least treble in ten years. I would suggest that £25,000 be invested in ten shares that conform to the criteria.

This will leave £5,000. Some might like to consider it a margin for enjoyment and work out their own investment plan. It will be good experience, it could be fun and it might well be profitable.

Finally, whenever a profit is realized, apply a part of it to pleasure, perhaps to self-indulgence, and almost certainly to charity. That is a very significant part of making money and remembering what life is all about. In real terms, a No Loss Portfolio must also include keeping one's values in perspective.

250 Per Cent Profit

It is planning not gambling that produces
profit and security.
Marcus Aurelius

The No Loss Portfolio offers some degree of flexibility, an opportunity for inventive speculation and even a margin for amusement. The 250 Per Cent Profit Plan was designed for those seeking guaranteed security and growth without any of the frills often associated with investment planning.

It was about 1975, when bucket-shop investment funds were thriving, that a man named Warren became disillusioned. The numerous investment schemes being offered by companies and individuals claiming to have the touch of Midas failed to impress him. Time and time again he listened to the excuses made by banks, fund managers and other optimists who only produced losses or, at best, marginal profits for their clients. But an analysis of the investment scene told Warren one positive fact which stood out above all others — there were thousands of people searching for a secure investment plan which could produce above-average capital appreciation. It was obvious that any such programme remotely related to equities would fall into the category of speculation. Equally, a purely insurance-oriented scheme would produce little more than the benefits readily available from dozens of reputable life insurance companies.

Checking out the various vehicles for investment planning, Warren hit upon one of the most successful ideas to emerge in recent times. The basis of the Plan is Government Gilt-Edged Securities coupled with a special life-assurance endowment policy, the latter mainly for its favourable tax treatment rather than the life-assurance element. This neat refinement makes the Plan available to investors up to the age of seventy-five, regardless of their state of health.

The Plan is successful mainly because of the effective way in which the original capital is securely invested. Practically the entire capital sum is applied to the purchase of a range of carefully selected Gilt-Edged Securities, the relatively small balance used to pay the first premium on a special ten-year policy. Future premiums are met from the guaranteed tax-free maturity values of the various Securities. After ten years the policy, with profits, matures to return a tax-free sum far in excess of any normal insurance contract or guaranteed investment scheme. Since the inception of the Warren Gilt Plan, investors have consistently enjoyed an appreciation of well over 250 per cent. And there is the added attraction that the Plan has absolutely no downside, provided that the investor stays with it for at least three years.

Partridge, Muir and Warren, who market the Plan, have produced many variations of the theme, all of which enable investors to provide substantial reserves for inheritance taxes, improve their immediate and long-term spendable incomes and provide unusually attractive benefits for children of all ages. In the field of planning worry-free secure investments, PMW have few competitors. The unusual combination of approved life-insurance policies and Government Stocks is unlikely to bring their Plans under attack from even the most left-wing government.

The unique strength of the principle involved lies in the combined benefits of two secure investments, both of which produce profits which are completely tax-free. There are few managed funds which have consistently performed as well over so long a period. Of those that might make such a claim, none can be certain that they will be able to maintain their profit record in the future — another factor that makes the Warren Plan attractive for those who seek to sleep at night and enjoy an above average return.

Bottoms Up Investment

No man needs more than one great idea to
be successful.

Don Marquis

Reputations and fortunes have been made by men who spot
obvious answers to apparently impossible problems. From
the time when Columbus cracked the bottom of an egg to
make it stand up to the complicated problems solved simply
by Edward de Bono, most men have continued to believe
that a complicated or difficult situation automatically
demands an answer to match. Generally, this is not so.

In the field of investment trusts, there have been few who
have made as much money as the operators. This is largely
due to the fact that fund managers, under whatever name,
have exactly the same facts and figures with which to play
the market as everyone else. Their genius is often illustrated
by their ability consistently to make the same excuses as
their colleagues. One conjures up a picture of hundreds of
fund managers having identical nightmares about the same
shares yo-yoing up and down the *Financial Times* Index;
one has visions of these same worried men and women
whispering over the asparagus, 'ICI is heading for a rise
because the Chancellor is due to make complimentary
remarks about the United States.' All the asparagus eaters
within earshot rush out, buy ICI shares and then tell their
friends, or write knowledgeable articles about it. The trouble
is that, in the meantime, more important news reaches the
Chancellor, who never gets around to speaking about the
US. Instead, he praises Germany for buying some of our new
ships. ICI shares promptly go down, but P & O shares rise.
Now comes the evidence that managers are inoculated with
the same dogma serum: instead of selling ICI and admitting
their mistake, they re-christen the share 'a medium-term
growth stock', and tip it as one to be held. This is the name
of the game which keeps many fund managers in business

and your money in limbo.

There are exceptions, because there are still men with imagination who do not rely on the crystal-ball gazers who write the City columns. Some years ago, Charles Fry, a London-based life-insurance broker became intrigued by the track record of some of the 'Worst Performing Investment Funds' managed by insurance companies and banks. Checking out a few dozen such funds over a period of some twenty years, Fry discovered a number of interesting facts. First, the vast majority of investors bought their units at or near the top of the market when share prices were at their highest. Second, few people wanted to buy or know anything about the poor-performing funds, regardless of why they may have made losses in any given year. Third, when loss-making units recovered they outperformed the market by a wide margin. Whichever way Fry drew his graph, the results were the same: amazing.

This is how a new investment programme was born. The concept was to take a group of reputable funds and chart the annual performance of the worst over a number of years. Initially, it was a hypothetical exercise. Fry would go through the motions of investing £10,000 in the fund shown at the bottom of the list. At the end of twelve months he would sell and invest in the new worst performer. The results were staggering. £10,000 invested in 1972 was worth £250,000 by 1985. Had the same sum been invested in the best performing funds, it would have realized just £25,000. A typical example was an American fund which fell heavily only because the dollar dropped against the pound by 40 per cent. In dollar terms it continued to do well and, when the dollar rose sharply, it outperformed most funds in the portfolio.

This relatively 'obvious' idea has made a fortune for Charles Fry and his large clientele. It had been staring a lot of people in the face for a long time. Regardless, however, of its proved success, a shake-up in the economy could still affect performance for a few years. A cautious investor should not place more than 20 per cent of his funds in this concept and should be prepared to leave it there for a number of years. Remember that a vindictive new govern-

ment could always play havoc with the equity market, and
the only way not to get hurt when some misguided politician pulls the rug is not to be on it. It should never be
forgotten that both unit and investment trusts are composed
of quoted securities, and in bad times they get hit as hard as
any. It is this fact that keeps the pessimists out of the market,
and it is the same fact that creates opportunities for the
optimists. In the arena of equity management, there are few
who have created formulae to compete with the 'Bottoms
Up Investment Plan'. As well as from the programme itself,
Charles Fry has continued to make money because he only
implements his idea with funds under top management.

Commodities

Pressure on the greed button frequently
anaesthetizes logical thinking.
Amos Hargraves Jnr

There can be few subjects that serve better to illustrate the
dividing line between gambling and investment than commodities, a term applied to goods which can be broadly
categorized as foodstuffs and raw materials. Apart from
grain, commodity markets tend to deal extensively in coffee,
tea, sugar, copper and other raw materials frequently
required in bulk by processors and consumers. Opportunities to trade in the immediate or short term are provided by
commodity exchanges where contracts are made to buy and
sell at agreed prices. The manufacturer who believes that tin
prices will rise over the next six months, will buy ahead in
the hope that he will profit as a result. On this basis he may
be required to pay only 10 per cent down as deposit until
the goods are due for delivery. In order to protect himself
against a possible fall in the market price of tin, the buyer
will simultaneously buy an option to sell, at the same price,
or marginally below it, a similar quantity to that bought in
his first contract. This is known as a futures contract. Thus,
if, between the purchase and the sale, the price of tin falls,
the buyer will be the one to lose on the first transaction but
will be the one who makes a profit on the futures transaction. For example, Mr A agrees a contract to buy ten tons
of tin at £1,000 a ton in three months' time; he sends his
broker £1,000 but has a liability for £10,000. To protect
himself, he enters into a second agreement to sell ten tons
at, say, £970 a ton, also in three months. If the price of tin
falls, he will still be obliged to complete the buying transaction — *but* he will be able to sell his option to sell at £970
a ton. In this way he could easily make a profit or, at worst,
suffer only a modest loss. (In addition, he would have to pay
a commission on each of the two contracts.)

Should the price of tin rise during the interim period, a profit would be made on the first transaction, and a loss on the futures contract.

This entire market operates because there are sufficient speculators who are prepared to play the market on their own account. It is a sophisticated world where varying prices in different exchanges create opportunities for the sharp-eyed and the experienced. In simple terms, the commodity exchange provides the means to trade without physical deliveries, and the futures market enables buyers and sellers to protect themselves against the risk of inordinate price changes. They are both establishments for professionals who understand the intricacies of the markets in which they trade and the basic and extraneous causes which produce demand and over-supply. When coffee plantations are destroyed by pests, prices of coffee rise, and when a substitute for sugar hits the headlines in America, the prices of sugar fall. But if it were as simple as that, commodity speculators would sleep at night and die of old age. They don't. Furthermore, most of their lay clients regret the day they ever heard of so-called investments in the commodity market. When a man buys £1,000 of shares and their value drops by 10 per cent, he loses £100. In the commodity market, he would use his £1,000 to buy £20,000 of copper. With a drop of only 5 per cent, the entire investment has been lost. That is the commodity market.

One of the most successful American commodity traders was Stanley Kroll, a man with a philosophy to which he stuck and about which he lectured and wrote books. He was knowledgeable, experienced and as cautious as any man can be in that market, and, like the top five per cent in any business, he had flair. It was this gut-feeling, that had long guided his activities in the market, that woke him up early one morning in a cold sweat. Suddenly, it came to him that a few points down in the wheat or pepper markets could wipe out the entire fortune he had made for himself. Kroll did not hang around and he did not spend any time re-reading the books he had written. He rushed to his office, and as soon as the exchanges opened he sold out every single bit of stock he was holding. He realized his assets in hard cash, paid off his staff, and closed the door on the business for all time. That same day he bought his wife a Rolls-Royce and said good bye to the commodity market. Some might say that his nerve had failed, but it would probably be more accurate to conclude that he saw the light. Once asked the secret of success in his business, he said, 'You gotta be bold and you gotta be right.' Asked what would happen if you were 'bold and wrong', he answered, 'So you go down with the ship.' Years after his retirement he confided that not one of his thousand private clients had ever made any real money out of commodity trading.

Years ago when the price of gold was down to around $35 an ounce there were some who gambled on its not falling any further. They were right, and those that hung on saw the price rise above $700 over a number of years. They were lucky: there were others who had considered the price was cheap at $750, and then watched the price tumble below $300. Unless one is a manufacturer, the commodity market is a game for masochists and gamblers, and the only way a small investor can make money out of it is to avoid it completely. How commodity unit trusts ever obtained authority to invite the public to participate must make one question the responsibility of those concerned. If, instead of buying 1,000 units, the little investor saw himself taking physical delivery of a ton of copper, he might appreciate how crazy he was to contemplate such an investment. Croupiers and commodity fund managers understand how to make money out of their clients — they should be seen in the same light. For those seeking guidance, invest in businesses you understand; leave cocoa for the chocolate manufacturers. Allowing for the fortunate and odd exception, the private speculator in commodity trading is more likely to make money from playing poker. There are those able to offset their losses against tax and they at least derive some pleasure in the knowledge that 60 per cent of the risk is carried by the Treasury.

Reversions

Success is just a matter of luck — ask any
failure.

Earl Wilson

Far away from the world of gambling, commodities and high
fliers, reversionary investments must rank among the more
sophisticated in the money market. A reversion is normally
an asset or share which offers relatively small return initially
because it has substantial potential in the future. A good
example is a property which was let at a fixed rent in 1969
for an unbroken period of twenty-one years. Assuming the
original rent was £10,000 a year, that is exactly what it will
remain at until it is reviewed in 1990. If by 1985 the market
rent, known as the rack rent, has increased to £30,000 a
year, there is a substantial reversionary value. This class of
investment has always appealed to the high taxpayer who is
concerned far more with capital growth than with income.
The profit on the reversion, if realized, will only attract Capital Gains Tax of 30 per cent after allowing for inflation
indexing. This could easily reduce the actual tax paid to 20
per cent over a medium term — distinctly attractive against
60 per cent, the top rate of income tax. It is surprising that
none of the property investment unit trusts have structured a
reversionary bond, particularly as such units could prove an
ideal lock-up for children and for those concerned only with
capital gains.

Although the term 'reversionary investment' is usually
associated with property, it can equally be applied in other
areas. A Government Stock may produce only a modest yield
because it stands well below the price at which it will be
redeemed at a given date. £100 of 3 per cent Treasury Stock
due for redemption in 1992 may well be priced at £70 six
years earlier. This is not likely to be of much interest to
someone who is looking to increase income. The capital

appreciation will, however, certainly be attractive to those seeking a guaranteed appreciation. This is particularly the case for people concerned with Capital Gains Tax liability — Government Stocks are not liable to any Capital Gains Tax whatsoever. As this tax is currently levied at 30 per cent for all capital profits over about £6,000 a year, the profit on Government Stocks is equivalent to 130 per cent on any other security.

Extending the principle to the share market requires a great deal more care and research. Many people have automatically assumed that a share with a very low yield must automatically have great growth potential. This, of course, can be the case. A property company that uses all its income to fund loans for future development will not be providing its shareholders with any return on capital until the new buildings are completed and let; at that time, of course, the shares can be expected to rise substantially. It is not uncommon, however, for the share price to discount this benefit one or two years ahead, for once it becomes generally known that the property could well affect the company's future profits, the share price will rise in anticipation before the development is completed. To avoid this problem an investor should ascertain the asset value per share of such a company before and after the proposed developments. It is not a difficult calculation to make and any stockbroker will have the figures readily to hand. The necessity to carry out this exercise has been highlighted many times, in particular in the high-flying computer world. A number of American computer shares rose from $20 to $200 on expectation, only to crash to $5 when the anticipated performance was not achieved.

In practice, a good reversion should be an investment where it is easy to recognize the capital growth potential, and a careful examination of, say, quoted Government and Company Securities can often disclose genuine opportunities. Of course, some might carry a degree of risk, and this needs to be taken into account before any purchase is made. The case of Loan Stock of the Port of London Authority is a good example. This 3 per cent loan is due to be repaid in full in 1999, the stock having been issued in 1929. In 1984 its price was around £33. This means that the stock was yielding a remarkable return of 9 per cent and in addition was guaranteed to produce a capital appreciation of 300 per cent in fifteen years — the only risk being that the Port of London Authority could go broke or be allowed to default in the meantime; failing that, this was probably one of the finest, most secure investments available. In addition, unlike property *per se*, it could also be cashed in at any time.

This is the type of investment which should form part of any sound, non-speculative portfolio. The only disadvantage to bear in mind is that prices will fluctuate with interest rates. If rates rise, the price of the loan stocks, like Gilts, will fall. If rates fall, then the prices will rise. This is, of course, of little importance to those mostly concerned with capital growth, who are prepared to hold the security until maturity if necessary.

The Best on the Market

I am not young enough to know everything.
James M. Barrie

There are no bankers, stockbrokers, insurance companies, financial institutions, fund managers, or others remotely connected with investments or financial advice, who do not read the *Financial Times* six days a week. Many will also study the *Wall Street Journal* and the *New York Herald Tribune.* To such people these publications, which provide up-to-date intelligence on the money world, are essential reading. Even an assistant to a junior stockbroker, whose opinion is only valued by his mother, is expected to treat the *FT* with the respect that other men reserve for their Prayer Book.

The fact remains that most of the regular readers of these excellent papers are not concerned with financial politics or intelligence but with company news, company results and the movement of share prices. Many are experts in the field; some are knowledgeable within certain limits; and large numbers are interested in the figures but relatively ignorant of the facts — these are the people who, like the majority with money problems and relatively modest investments, want to find information and guidance. The pundits in the Sunday press may well offer useful share advice on companies that will be going somewhere this year or next, but the reader still does not know how to examine his own financial position. Odd references to tax-efficient investments, family trusts and fixed-interest securities leave the average reader little the wiser. He desperately needs an unbiased guide, written in simple language, to help him understand the workings of investment trusts, the advantages of woodland investments and the taxation implications of unauthorized unit trusts.

Fortunately, such a guide exists. Unlike this book, which is intended to cover a very broad and undefined spectrum of

money-oriented subjects, *Investment Guide* is a serious
annual, consisting of some 250 pages of well-documented,
highly relevant and topical easy reading. Its scope is vast, its
presentation professional, and it is updated each year. The
fact that it is produced and edited by those closely
associated with the Allied Dunbar Insurance Group is almost
irrelevant.

For those interested in understanding the investment
scene and the tax aspects of personal money management, it
is essential reading.

A Rose By Any Other Name

All you need to lose money in this life is
ignorance and confidence.

Mark Twain

Over the years, simple expressions have been given fresh
meaning when voiced by investment consultants, stockbrokers and city editors. The following examples are for
those with market amnesia who might profit by tempering
their excessive enthusiasm with a little cynicism.

EXPRESSION	DEFINITION
Widows' and Orphans' Shares	Ideal for those who are defenceless.
Gilt-Edged Stock	Unlikely to depreciate in value faster than the £.
Growth Stocks	In good times, these are the shares that should not go down further.
Portfolio Manager	A professional illusionist in the stock market. Unlike the croupier, he places the bets and spins the wheel.
Recovery Stock	A share that should do well if the orders arrive before the receiver.
The institutions are buying	Fund managers now believe that shares will depreciate more slowly than cash.
Shares for Capital Appreciation	Benevolent term for shares with a low yield.
City Editor	A frustrated clairvoyant

	aspiring to be an evangelist for capitalism.
Financial Times Index	An indicator as helpful to the average investor as a sundial to an airline pilot.
The share is a short-term investment	Your stockbroker has also bought a few.
This is a take-over situation	A big client is selling.
Knowledgeable people are buying	Knowledgeable people are selling.
One of the big banks is buying	The bankers are worried about the overdraft.
Pension funds are not selling this share	They can afford to take a ten-year view.
This share will react well to a reduction in interest rates	The company is about to miss a dividend payment.
The company is known to be diversifying	It can't face the competition. Even the bailiffs are worried.
They supply the big stores	They work on small margins.
The US are their biggest customers	They're worried about the dollar.
It's good for a charitable trust	The share is ex-growth.
The company is bringing out a new model	They have over-spent.
The company is going to have a Rights issue	The directors can't face the bank.
The accountants have qualified the accounts	The accountants are worried they'll be sued for negligence.
The Chairman has resigned	The board has lost confidence.

The price has doubled	SELL!
but the share is still	
worth buying	

The abundance of optimism often reflected in stock-market terminology might aptly be described as financial romanticism that has lost its reason. Douglas Jerrold once said that luck could make even madness wisdom. History shows that most men need more luck than that to make a fortune from trading in stocks and shares.

TURNING AN
HONEST PENNY

The Little Business

*The gambling known as business looks with
austere disfavour upon the business known as
gambling.*

Ambrose Bierce

Every year, thousands of people try to supplement the family
income by starting a little business. Inspired by tales of
success, and guided by hope or misleading advertisements,
they launch themselves onto the fringe of the commercial
jungle. Room for their enterprise is readily provided by
those who had similar aspirations a year or two earlier and
have retreated wiser, sadder and, too often, poorer.

At best, the rewards from mail-order promises and the like
are disappointing for anyone hoping to make more than
pocket money in their spare time. Little boutiques, car-wash
equipment, catalogue sales and wine agencies all sound
attractive, so long as overheads are underestimated and the
time factor ignored. Ideally, one should look for a business
which requires no staff outside the family, no stock-piling,
no additional premises and no cash outlay beyond a nominal figure. In this way it should be possible to calculate the
downside accurately without having to speculate with any
real, hard-earned capital.

It has been successfully shown that the following

approach can create the maximum dividends with the minimum risk. The potential ill-effects on the family are practically nil and the initial financial commitment can be nominal.
The Six Rules of SLIP — the Supplementary Little Investment
Plan — are simple but important:

1   Decide what the maximum amount of time is that
you and your spouse can afford to devote to your new
business. Then, halve it! Most people are carried away by
enthusiasm when making their first estimates.

2   Remember that you have each other, you have a
home, you have a family. The initial intention is to supplement your income, not to make a fortune at the expense
of your marriage or your family.

3   Consider carefully the maximum amount of capital
you can afford to *lose*. For this purpose, all loans and
bank borrowings should be ignored. Then, make up your
mind that this is your working capital until the business
starts to tick over.

4   Consider the additional income you believe you
need to enjoy the standard of living you would like to
achieve. Then double it. The additional amount represents your challenge and your real profit.

5   Make up your mind to pay all bills promptly.

6   Avoid any business that involves giving credit.

Choosing a Business

1   Make up your mind to operate from home. If the
ideal place is your garage, check that your car is fully
insured as it will have to be left out all night.

2   Choose an object the production of which can easily
be sub-contracted to retired craftsmen or handymen or
housewives.

3   Aim at a business which will bring you into direct
competition with a manufacturer who you would expect
to have large overheads. Consider if it is possible to operate a similar business on a smaller scale.

4   Write and re-write exactly how you see your operation working. Build a programme which precisely covers
the timing and financing of your purchases, your out-

workers, your collections, deliveries and payments on account. The accent should always be on economy of both time and expenditure but not on quality.

To illustrate the last point, take a very simple television table, which costs a retailer £20, and which he sells for £30. It is reasonable to assume that the manufacturer produces the table for £14 and aims to make a net profit of £2-£3, allowing for the cost of rent, materials, labour, production, delivery charges and advertising. To compete, an unknown supplier would probably need to supply his table for no more than £16. This is a distinct possibility, bearing in mind that, working from a garage with no paid staff, there are practically no overheads. If the sums look like the following, then one is in business:

Per table

Raw materials and labour	£9.00
Delivery charges and telephone calls	.20
Postage and petrol	.30
Margin for error	2.00
Profit	3.50
Selling price to retailer	£15.00

On this basis there is a more than adequate margin for increased costs of labour and materials, and for possible discounts for larger orders.

In the event, a couple who went ahead with this SLIP in the North of England discovered that they had over-estimated and certainly did not need the margin. They had taken the following steps:

1   They bought a TV table and carefully took it to pieces.
2   They improved the design slightly as to make it serve equally well as a coffee table.
3   The man drew precise plans for each piece and got the local timber yard to cut wood exactly to size.
4   Without rushing the job, the man sandpapered and

assembled the pieces, making a note of the time taken.

5   He showed the finished table to the buyer of a local furniture store and established that the store would readily pay £16 for it.

6   Next he advertised in a *local* newspaper for retired handymen interested in working at home. He was inundated with applications.

7   The couple then visited the handymen nearest to their home. After seeing samples of their craft, they agreed to pay a fixed amount for each table assembled.

8   During the following week, the wife offered the table to retailers within a radius of five miles from their home. Her terms were strictly cash on delivery. The orders began to arrive.

9   Together, the couple visited a local chartered accountant. He outlined the details of all the tax implications involved in their business and advised them to discuss their new venture with their bank manager.

10   They formed a limited company with a capital of £100. Being convinced that the business would be successful, they placed 50 per cent of the shares in trust for their children.

11   At first, the man collected and delivered the tables himself at weekends. Subsequently, he employed a local firm to collect and deliver all the raw materials as well as the tables. He and his wife always collected the money themselves.

12   Orders for the table parts were placed with several different timber yards, so that the business would not be dependent on a single supplier. Furthermore, this reduced the chances of creating competition. The timber yards were happy to give fourteen days' credit, which was more than adequate.

13   The initial target was to make and sell fifty tables a week. This was achieved within a few months. In the first year the business made a pre-tax profit of £6,000. Within three years an enterprise which had started with under £200 at risk was earning over £45,000 per annum. As a result, the wife has an independent income, the second car is no burden and the children's trust pays for school

fees and holidays. More important, the couple still enjoy a full family life.

This is what SLIP is all about: planning a small business with the minimum expenditure of time and capital. There is no doubt that this operation can be applied equally successfully to numerous products which are normally manufactured in expensive factories with high overheads. Good examples include garden furniture, casual clothing, picture frames, light fittings, leather goods and small items for the car and home — the best places to look for ideas are large department stores, chemists, furniture shops and the mail-order pages of the better magazines. With an increasing number of able people retiring early, there is no shortage of labour in most areas.

The following golden rules are always worth observing:

AVOID
1   Mass-produced, cheap items with only nominal profit margins.
2   Specialist suppliers of raw materials who can let you down — e.g., importers and foreign manufacturers.
3   Customers who insist on credit. Offer a discount if necessary but do not go into competition with the banks.
4   Articles which require considerable expertise in their production.
5   Demands which could impose pressure on your bank balance, your family or too much of your weekends.
6   Giving away your business secrets. This is of great importance — remember, your aim is to create profits, not competition.

The Franchise Business

*Some people use half their ingenuity to get
into debt and the other half staying in it.*
                       George D. Prentice

There are no reliable statistics to show the numbers of
people who have been made or ruined by entering the franchise business. This is a marketing industry which can, at its
best, provide profitable opportunities for those with some
capital who want to start from the second rung of the lad-
der. For others, who are too often driven by enthusiasm
alone, it can easily create short-term illusions and long-term
distress.

The secret of successful franchise operations, from the
point of view of the franchisors, is the devout spreading of
the Gospel of Profit without Effort. There is never a shortage
of those who desperately want to believe the Message of
Midas, which is probably the easiest religion in the world to
sell. The franchisees are already converted to the Faith and
only await their Messiah.

The blind acceptance of the Theology of Instant Wealth
has also often led thousands of innocent people to buy
shares in non-existent cattle, heavily diluted perfume and
unmarketable postage stamps. They are the same people
who are easily persuaded to invest in car-cosmetic units
sited in derelict slums, unbuilt overseas chalets, Taiwan
jewellery, off-beat photographic kiosks and other 'formulas
for success' which have brought moments of grandeur and
years of self-reproach. And they buy franchises.

There are, of course, franchise offers which are genuine
and do justify careful consideration. The following guide is
designed to help the inexperienced and the unsuspecting
save time, distress and capital.

1   If you doubt the validity of any franchise offer, do
not attempt to justify it. Simply forget it.

2   If you really like the idea, be very careful. First take

the opinion of an experienced business friend. Second, consult an accountant or a lawyer and offer to pay for a 'devil's advocate' report (one that points out all the downside aspects of the proposition). The fees you pay for this could well be your best investment.

3   If the report advises you against the deal, accept the counsel you have paid for — do not question it or discuss it with the franchise promotors.

4   If the report is encouraging, request a list of customers from the franchisors, and follow up at least six. Choose those who have been operating their own franchise for a minimum of a year. They are the ones who have had the time to discover the pitfalls.

5   Should this exercise raise any real doubts in your mind, do not pursue the matter any further. Never be a guinea-pig in the franchise business.

6   If all your investigations come up trumps, you have probably found a worthwhile opportunity. At this stage, take it to your bank manager to discuss finance. If he is prepared to provide the capital you need, you are doing well — but do not deposit your house as security unless the amount involved is truly modest. As a final precaution, discount the estimated profits. If the deal still looks even reasonable — good luck.

Final Warnings

Never borrow more than a modest percentage of the capital required to purchase a franchise, particularly if you have no previous experience in the business.

If a franchise involves renting a shop, check the shopping parade and adjoining streets carefully. It is important to have neighbours who are already attracting the type of customer you will need for your own business. Run a mile from any suggestion that a new shopping precinct is to be built a few hundred yards away.

Penny Wise

Some opportunities start small.

Anon.

The last farthing ever to be produced was minted in 1956. In that year a man walked into his bank and bought 96,000 mint farthings for £100. He gave them to his young son and forgot about them. Twenty years later, in 1976, that investment was worth over £60,000 — roughly what he could have expected from a bank-maintained investment of £30,000 in the companies comprising the *Financial Times* Index. It should be added that had the coins been anything but in mint condition the investment would have yielded substantially less.

Some people may, understandably, doubt that such investments could ever be repeated, and they will happily continue to back horses and play bingo. Some, on the other hand, may take the view that over the years small coins are continually being taken out of circulation, and history might easily repeat itself. The ½p has already gone, and while it would be over-optimistic to expect any sudden appreciation, over the years, every mint coin will become a collector's piece. In commercial terms, the current new-penny piece is already a nuisance, and it is almost bound to follow its half-brother within the next few years. A few pounds invested for grandchildren could well prove worthwhile; and in the year that the penny is due to be taken out of circulation, it may be a reasonable gamble to double up on the investment — but you should buy the coins only in mint condition, and you must be prepared to wait a generation for any reasonable profit.

Coins should be considered a long-shot investment but there are hundreds of thousands of collectors throughout the world and the numbers continue to increase. Historically, carefully chosen coins, in mint condition, have proved outstanding long-term investments. It is interesting to compare the investment of £500 in an insurance-oriented scheme in 1965 with the same amount invested in mint half-crowns. Twenty years later the insurance investment was worth £1,200 — the half-crowns had a value close to £20,000.

This does not mean that one should buy coins indiscriminately but, over the long term, mint coins have produced excellent returns. If one is contemplating anything other than a modest investment, it is probably best to consider it a serious hobby and compare the advice of several coin collectors before buying.

Who Buys Retail?

Do other men for they would do you.
Charles Dickens

The chairman of a multimillion-pound chain-store is said to have defined a fool as a man who buys retail. This may well be apocryphal but there is certainly more than an element of truth in the statement.

Starting at the top end of the market, it is doubtful if there is a single jeweller in Bond Street or Fifth Avenue who would refuse to give a discount on a worthwhile purchase. Invariably the profit margins are such that no customer would be allowed to walk out of a shop simply because he or she offered 10 to 15 per cent less than the quoted price. On an article retailed at £2,000 a customer could save £300 — a top-rate taxpayer would need to earn an additional £750 a year to have an extra net £300 — and this saving is available just for the asking. There are well-known jewellers throughout all major cities who have built their businesses on granting discounts indiscriminately — with their retail prices based on mark-ups of 35 to over 100 per cent, such concessions are worth their while. No insurance company ever replaces a piece of jewellery or *objet d'art* at its retail price. No insurance assessor would dare tell his principal that he was unable to negotiate a discount of at least 10 per cent.

It is difficult to believe that the majority of private car buyers still pay the full retail price (usually marked up by about 20 per cent) when purchasing a new vehicle; it does not make sense when any business house in the country can obtain a saving of 10 to 15 per cent. This must be real money to most people spending thousands of pounds on a new car: on a £10,000 car, for instance, a discount of twelve per cent represents a net saving of £1,200. Furthermore, if English people care to take the trouble to buy their cars on the Continent and drive them back, the saving can be even more substantial, because of the difference between the tax systems of the two countries. It must be admitted, however, that it is easier and less time-consuming to go to the car-dealer round the corner.

In the 1970s an American visitor to London was offered a Renoir painting by an art dealer in St James's for £15,000. This was very cheap, even though Renoirs were not selling very well in that year. But bank interest rates were around 18 per cent and the American calculated that the dealer, who had probably paid no more than £10,000, would be pleased to make a sale at any price that put money in his bank account. He offered £12,000 and when this was refused he began to walk away. He got the Renoir for £12,000, and the dealer has been treating him as a valued client ever since.

Those who still nurture reservations should remember that retailers in the above trades expect customers to seek a reduction: they have usually allowed for it in the price. Works of art, jewellery, antiques, furs, expensive clothes and cars are probably the best examples where discounts can be readily obtained but almost any article falls into this category. The only rule of thumb to follow is to restrict bargaining to values that are important to the vendor. A man who once tried to obtain a discount on a relatively small and cheap item in an antique shop was asked by the elderly shop-owner whether the item was for himself or a gift; learning that it was the latter, the owner then said, 'That's all very well, but why should I contribute to a present for your friend?'

Insurance companies, too, grant discounts, or agencies, and there is not a major corporation anywhere that does not enjoy some financial benefit from those handling their insurance. Furthermore, ethics in that business are such that most insurers, with the exception of Lloyd's, will bend their words and their bonds to give a direct agency to a large account. Fortunately — for the brokers — as insurance companies can rarely offer unbiased advice, the insured is obliged to use an intermediary and thus receive a lower discount. It would be fair to add that most reputable brokers adopt an indignant moral stance to this practice — at least in the case of accounts producing premiums below, let us say, £100,000.

Small is Beautiful

Making money can be fun, and after a certain
point it can bring more money.

Neil Simon

Some people do not read the *Financial Times*, the City
columns or the *Wall Street Journal*. They do not have a
stockbroker, and neither do they listen to stock-market talk
and tales of those who made, or nearly made, a fortune.
They do not build or inherit large businesses. Yet they make
a great deal of money without speculating with substantial
sums or exploiting the innocent.

They think and the process of their thoughts run along
the following lines:

1   I own my own house.
2   I am staying in my job because I like it, or because it
is not convenient to leave it.
3   I cannot make any worthwhile capital from my net
income.
4   I do not understand the stock market and I do not
have confidence in those who claim to.
5   At best I can expect a relatively modest profit from
insurance schemes or other safe forms of investment. It is
possible that none of them will keep pace with inflation —
so in real terms I could be losing money.
6   What can I buy which should increase in value
because there will come to be a demand for it, or because
for some special reason its value will appreciate? Such
items should be small as I have no storage space.

They realize that small, fine works of art can today rarely
be produced at the prices at which older items of decorative
art can be purchased. They correctly assume that,
somewhere in the world, there will always be people with a
desire to own unusual, beautiful objects. They also know
only too well that they are not progressing through an

original thought process; so they decide to look for articles that are currently out of fashion or have for some unaccountable reason been overlooked.

Not many years ago, a man spent his leisure time pottering around antique shops hoping to spot something that was cheap, pretty and beautifully made. After a few months he found a hand-painted Chinese snuff-bottle which he bought for £3. It was quite obvious that this magnificent example of Oriental art could never be made again for anything like the price. Over the next two years he read a great deal and asked a lot of questions about Chinese snuff-bottles. He built up a small collection at a total cost of £1,000, and catalogued each item. Within ten years he had sold his original purchases for over £20,000, keeping back his more expensive items believing that they were going to appreciate more substantially. He was right. Not many years afterwards he made a second sale for £100,000. By that time, Chinese snuff-bottles were big business and he stopped buying them.

Instead he looked for another object which had not yet gained popularity. He kept his eyes open, and read English and American journals which specialized in unusual, second-hand goods rather than antiques. It was not long before he was quietly investing in eighteenth-century hand-painted American tobacco jars, another overlooked collector's item.

The possibilities are still endless. Paper knives, fans, keys, bookmarks, manicure sets, greetings cards, pens, shaving mugs, watches, photo frames, combs, old business receipts, indentures, tavern menus, spectacles, early models of cycles, small pieces of Victorian furniture, tie-pins, walking-sticks, visiting-card cases, locks, shirt-studs — virtually any old and interesting or attractive item which might make an interesting collection or adorn a shelf or corner in a comfortable home. The following tips might be borne in mind:

1   Take your time.
2   Choose an item likely to have an international appeal.

3   Only buy perfect specimens; they are the ones that stand a real chance of appreciating in value.

4   Do your best to read up on the history of each article so that you become an expert on it. If the necessary books are not readily available from bookshops or your local library, contact the British Library for guidance. It is important that you should acquire enough knowledge to tell whether you are buying something made in, say, the eighteenth or nineteenth century or whether it is a later imitation.

5   Do not buy in a hurry if you have the slightest doubt.

6   Do not expect to find bargains in expensive antique shops. The likely hunting grounds are markets, shops in country villages and small auctions advertised in local papers.

7   Remember that you are investing not trading. Initially, think of it as a hobby-with-potential rather than a business and only buy things you like − of course, if you like them very much, you may become an avid collector rather than an investor.

8   As you will be taking a longer view than most, you can afford to pay a little more for quality.

9   Never buy with money you are likely to need in a hurry.

10   Whenever you buy from a dealer, always appear naive. You learn more that way. But no dealer ever expects to sell at his asking price, so never be afraid to bargain − the dealer also makes his living that way.

This whole concept may not produce the excitement derived from backing horses or playing the stock market but it is certainly likely to develop into a fascinating interest with far better chances of long-term profit and without the potential of short-term distress and aggravation.

Worth the Paper it's Printed On

It can take twenty years to make an overnight
success.

Eddie Cantor

Not so many years ago, a few people in different parts of the
world became bored with coins and began collecting old
banknotes. Soon afterwards, one of these enthusiastic
characters wrote a book about the subject. It was certainly
not a literary masterpiece, and it received relatively little
publicity, but it was responsible for launching another
hobby. At that time philatelists and others laughed at the
author and held his ideas up to ridicule. Within a few years,
however, much obsolete paper currency was worth many
times its original face value. Collectors numbered in their
thousands, catalogues were produced by the dozen, and a
simple amusing hobby became an investment industry.
By that time the author of that book had become a very
wealthy man and his erstwhile critics were laughing *with*
him.

The wisdom of getting on this band-wagon at this stage is
perhaps doubtful, but only a few years ago another hobby
was born in the United Kingdom. Quite suddenly, old bonds
became a vogue. Years ago these had been issued by
governments and large corporations to raise money for
railroads and other utilities. Subsequently, they were repaid
or became quite valueless. In the event, it was considered to
have sufficient potential as an investment hobby for Stanley
Gibbons, the leading firm of stamp dealers, to open a
department specializing in encouraging a new breed of
collectors to recognize yet another collecting interest.

Many of these old bonds were so beautifully designed
that scores of people have had them framed to hang on their
walls while waiting for their investment potential to be
realized. Whether collectors will ever make the sort of
money that has been made from rare stamps and banknotes

remains to be seen. Busted bonds that are bought for fun might one day paper your garden shed, or they might pay for a new house. That is the only way to think when buying them.

Late Payment

Running into debt isn't so bad. It's running
into creditors that hurts.

J.M. Braude

Apart from necessity, it is often habit or philosophy or
cunning which makes private individuals late payers. The
first category simply cannot manage their budget and rely on
deferring the settlement of bills, many of them surviving by
mastering the art of manufacturing a steady flow of original
excuses for delaying payment. The second category settle all
accounts at the last moment in the same way as they
consistently arrive at railway stations as the guard is about to
blow his whistle; they are the people who grope for their
theatre seats two minutes after the curtain rises. The third
group firmly believe they have a divine right to keep
creditors waiting, regardless of whether they are the garage,
the chemist, the local authority or the Church. Some of them
have decided only to settle bills one day a month, and any
bill that arrives the following day or thereafter can wait up to
a further thirty days for settlement. Their excuse is simply to
announce that they are made that way. Finally, there are
those who hope the bills might be overlooked or that a
percentage of their creditors will consider it not worth their
while to sue. They know that, in many cases, firms will send
out just one solicitor's letter before writing off their small
debts. It is those of this class who 'accidentally' post-date or
fail to sign cheques, or claim that goods or services were not
up to standard.

These are the four categories that haunt every trader,
produce blood-pressure casualties and undermine faith in
human nature. Some, although they are akin to parasites,
create sympathy at one extreme; while some bring out the
worst in people at the other. One such late payer, known to
query every bill and then defer settlement, was Oscar Wilde;
but, then, he lived beyond his means — and, when he was

confronted with the prospect of an expensive operation, he sighed, 'Ah, well, then, I suppose that I shall have to die beyond my means.' By and large, paying late is a joke to some, an aggravation to most and a subject on which a sanctimonious minority pontificate.

But there is, of course, another side to the coin. Contrary to popular belief, banks simply love reliable clients who pay late and run up overdrafts. Unlike the good, steady, always-in-the-black client, the customer with the overdraft is the one who produces the best profits. He is also likely to receive the most attention and have the opportunity of building up a reputation as a reliable borrower. Properly monitored, it is he who produces the steady 20-per cent-plus return on his bank credit-card account and compensates for the mean client who pays promptly expecting the banks to be satisfied with the profit of 5 per cent which they extract from retailers.

There are those who have amassed fortunes pandering to the whims of late-payers. A well-known clothing manufacturer, for instance, added twelve months' interest to his normal price and then granted six months' credit terms to all his retailers who were prepared to send post-dated cheques by return. A specialist banker was happy to discount the interest on these cheques, leaving the manufacturer with his normal profit plus a net 4 per cent risk-free. By choosing the retailers carefully, there were practically no bad debts and all concerned were happy. The manufacturer trebled his business without the agony of financing his customers, the retailers were able to increase their turnover without prejudicing their bank overdraft facilities and the discount bank enjoyed the benefits of a substantial new account.

Banks and some businesses can make money from late payers, but as a rule — particularly those without the means to chase up accounts — the majority should steer well clear of those who for any reason make a practice of settling accounts unduly late: all too often, lack of credit control has been directly responsible for bankruptcy.

When I'm Sixty-Five

The only difference between a grave and a rut
are the dimensions.

Will Rogers

Age, accident, illness or redundancy compel thousands to
change their life-styles every year. Suddenly, people previously considered utterly indispensable become readily
disposable. Whether top executives or steelworkers, people
who over the years had become accustomed to travelling
effortlessly in high gear are suddenly obliged to get off the
track.

Some try desperately hard to come to terms with their
changed circumstances, their lower income and their free
time. Others endeavour to stretch themselves in fresh
employment, but too often shock, fear and over-reaction
clouds good judement. Too many people fail to take the
opportunity to assess their maximum potential in an area of
change.

The first consideration should be to recognize the order
of priorities. If, for example, immediate or gradual physical
immobility is inevitable, moving the bedroom from the first
floor to the ground floor is not a satisfactory answer. It is far
more practical and less traumatic to move to a bungalow or
a flat. This kind of constructive acknowledgement of change
places a man or woman ahead of the game. The first action
is a form of intellectual and physical resignation, the second
frequently enables the individual to defer making serious
changes in many day-to-day activities, and has the psycho-
logical benefit that lies in rising to a challenge. The person
who concentrates on remaining mentally alert is winning
and any plan that encourages this must be worth following,
always assuming that it is not imposing undue financial
strain.

At this stage the answers to the following questions are
relevant:

1   If able, would you be happy to take a local job
     on a lower scale than previously?   Yes/No
2   If you are virtually housebound, would you still
     like a commercial involvement?   Yes/No
3   Would you really like to face a
     fresh challenge?   Yes/No
4   Do you want to continue to make money?   Yes/No
5   Do you believe you and your spouse could
     work well together?   Yes/No
6   Would you really prefer to potter?   Yes/No

Score:

1   Yes 5   No 10
2   Yes 10   No 5
3   Yes 10   No 0
4   Yes 10   No 5
5   Yes 20   No 5
6   Yes 5   No 10

If your score is under 45, you might consider charity
work, writing that book you have always had in mind — or
becoming an avid television viewer. You may well have
decided, quite rightly, to step off the merry-go-round, at
least for the time being. Ask yourself the questions again in
three months' time.

If you score over 45, bear in mind that the answer to
question 5 could be the most significant.

The next priority is to accept that you are starting a new
life, possibly with limitations but, more likely, with fresh
opportunities. You may no longer be concerned with top-
level negotiations, mass-production figures or long-distance
travel, but that could all be to your advantage; now, you are
able to think afresh. Even if you are seeking full-time
employment, you should try to keep yourself happily occupied with something that is neither physically nor financially
too demanding. Ideally, it should be something that interests
you and stands a reasonable chance of generating a useful
additional income without much risk.

For a potential business idea to pass the test, the following conditions should be considered essential:

1   It should not require your home to be used as a store or warehouse.

2   It should not encourage too many telephone calls or visits.

3   Except for your spouse, if he or she is genuinely interested, your new home-business should not involve partnerships. The risks of misunderstandings are usually too great.

4   It should not be concerned with franchise arrangements. They require capital investment and are usually too demanding.

5   It should not involve substantial volume packaging.

6   It should not necessitate giving credit.

7   Do not make your decision in a hurry.

8   Do not plan to borrow money.

Simply to tune into the idea of small-business thinking, buy a copy of *Exchange & Mart* and read it slowly. Boring it might be, but it is always full of opportunities and something may suggest itself to you. Even the sort of business which would not normally even enter your head may become interesting if approached from a slightly different angle. For example, bulk-buying of foreign stamps for sale in small packages may be hackneyed in the UK, but it might well have potential for exporting to, say, Switzerland, where the pound may be cheap. Each time you imagine you have come up with a bright idea check whether it meets the following criteria:

1   You believe you could cope with the competition, if any.

2   You would not be dependent on the gullibility of your customers.

3   It has possibilities of growing as a steady on-going business without creating excessive demands.

4   You will enjoy it.

5   You will be able to cope in the time you can comfortably devote to it.

6   Your conservative calculations indicate that the financial potential justifies the effort.

If nothing at all in *Exchange & Mart* strikes a chord, remember that you are only looking for an idea, so go through the process a few times over, and take your time. Repeat the performance with other magazines and catalogues. You are now no longer living on your memories, you have moved into a new creative phase.

Whatever you ultimately decide to do, make up your mind that, so long as you are sufficiently fit, mentally and physically, you will plan each day. Maybe you will start a business, give your garden more time, assist at the local hospital, join the bowls club or the local drama group, enrol for a course of study — whatever you do, the single important thing to remember is that inactivity is a formula for premature senility.

Profits from Emotions

The advantages of emotions is that they lead
us astray.

Oscar Wilde

Consideration might well be usefully given to filling needs
which carry no specific price tags and are not advertised in
magazines. The world is full of people who nurture hopes,
dreams and affections which offer enormous scope for
honest, commercial exploitation.

In America, there are upwards of thirty million cat-loving
people, apart from ordinary common or garden cat-owners.
These folk treat their pets like children or companions; they
send them birthday cards and Christmas presents; every year
they write countless letters to newspapers and magazines
about the wonders and habits of their cats. A percentage of
these people may well be thrilled at the thought of joining
an Anglo-American cat-lovers club. As a commercial venture,
this theme can be dismissed, or, alternatively, it can be
developed in many ways in many geographical areas. If the
idea appeals to you, then cost your overheads very carefully.
You could test it by inserting small advertisements in the
Personal Columns of *The Times* and *Cat Fancy*, the American cat magazine — those genuinely interested will happily
enclose stamped addressed envelopes with their enquiries.
Initially, an annual subscription might be charged for a quar-
terly newsletter and information on goods, services and
hints for cat-lovers. Manufacturers and distributors of such
material would happily grant special terms to all members of
the club, and probably take regular advertising space in the
newsletter as well.

Among the population of Hong Kong are some 300-
400,000 expatriates, many of whom feel more British than
the people who live in the United Kingdom; and many of
whom still believe Britain has an Empire and talk with a
patriotism and enthusiasm that is a credit to the Royal

Family. Any links with the Old Country are precious, and fresh personal or material associations become treasures overnight.

It is conceivable that prints of different counties, churches or colleges might have an enormous appeal to many who would be happy to adorn their walls with reminders of home or their youth. One print leads to another and Hong Kong might well be a market for a million small, large, coloured and black-and-white prints. Colonials are used to paying in advance, prints can be posted safely in envelopes and the business could offer boundless opportunities for development. Once again, use the Personal Columns to advertise for both customers and distributors. Think before you plan, and consider area agents, rather than direct customers, in order to cut down administration and develop goodwill more quickly. If your advertisements do not produce the right enquiries, write to the commercial attaché of the British Embassy. His job is to be helpful, and he invariably is. Check other countries for similar arrangements. A fairly high profit margin will be acceptable if everything else is right.

It is a business idea which is unlikely to attract many callers, so there is potential there; furthermore, you can readily acquire expertise and move at your own pace. But you will still have to work at it.

Of course it is ideal if you can combine a business with a hobby. All over the world there are those who assiduously collect the letters and autographs of famous people. Generating stock in this field may well prove time-consuming and expensive, but there is a vast market simply waiting. A little research will produce a substantial list of fan-clubs which revel in keeping alive memories of celebrities, including many who have long been forgotten by the majority of people. America is knee-deep in such societies, and they are often delighted to pay high prices for anything which can be added to their mini-museums. Who could have imagined, twenty years ago, that ten million T-shirts would sell at ten times their cost simply because they carry the picture of a singer who couldn't read music, let alone sing in tune. Today, it is no longer newsworthy.

Allegedly, there is an order of ladies dedicated to perpetuating the name of Florence Nightingale; a choral society with
a Caruso library, a Keyser II club, and a group of antique
silver enthusiasts who are still thrilled by anything
connected with Hester Bateman, the Georgian lady silver-
smith. As for Dickens, Shakespeare, Chaucer, Milton, Kipling,
Mark Twain and countless other literary figures, the world is
full of societies set up in their memory, and many of them
publish regular news-sheets.

The potential is endless, particularly as the business does
not appear to be over-crowded. A word of warning, however
— the Law of Copyright applies to letters and, legally, one is
obliged to wait until an individual has been dead for fifty
years before trading in his correspondence or his writings;
but this barely limits the scope of the exercise.

Note your ideas in a special notebook, leaving a page to
develop each fresh thought. If you have the capacity to
produce practical and potentially profitable ideas, in depth,
you might even start a business selling ideas. Whatever you
do, though, do not sell them cheaply. Nobody will thank
you or respect you for under-pricing your good ideas.

Idea Production

A word has been known to destroy a man's
life. An idea has built a nation.
Norman Ford

Imaginative people recognize that boredom or even redundancy can be a signal for some to move into reverse gear and
for others to re-assess or create opportunities.

To create an opportunity, you need first to have an idea,
and then to develop it. The following provides an outline for
documenting a practical idea designed to fill a specific need.
The figures quoted, and the names mentioned, are for illustration purposes only.

Documenting a New Business Idea

Business idea   Service to expatriates.

Potential market 1,500,000 people (confirmed by Foreign
Office).

Approximate income bracket   Medium to high.

Possible needs   UK-oriented objects not readily available
locally.
Information on schools.
Information on providing school fees.
Housing problems.
Hotel and holiday information.
Ultimate retirement in UK.
Problems of repatriation.
Investment opportunities.

Likely sources of information   Foreign Office, Board of
Trade, Embassies, Commercial Attachés,
international accountants and lawyers, the
Press Association, and information depart-

ments of newspapers like *The Times* and the *Telegraph*.

First thought for the idea Providing a reminder service for birthdays, anniversaries, etc.

Conclusion Insufficient profit potential.

Second thought Private school fees service.

Conclusion Market well covered.

Third thought Retirement in the UK. Information indicates that 150,000 will eventually return to live in the UK. That means that a large number will be looking for new homes. These people will probably have amassed substantial savings, having worked for years in low-tax zones.

Thought process Is there a way of encouraging a percentage to buy a house years before they require it on the grounds that it will ultimately produce a considerable saving? Such people must be returning to the UK every year, looking for houses to buy. Would it be possible to encourage at least 200 people to pay £100 a year for a specialist home-buying service? Would a number of major companies pay £1,000 a year for the service for their staff?

Develop specialist advice Where is specialist advice and intelligence available? Home magazines, *Estates Gazette* and local newspapers, etc.

Consider areas where people overseas prefer to return to: a) to continue working, and b) to retire.

Buy copies of local papers from at least ten major cities, such as Leeds, Manchester, London, as these are the places where people may well return to work; and from a number of towns like Bournemouth,

Brighton or Worthing, traditionally retirement centres. From these papers, you should be able to put together and index a realistic list of comparative prices. Additional information should be readily available from local estate agents, with whom a mutually advantageous relationship could be set up. Establish immediately that you will expect 25 per cent of all fees and commissions they receive directly or indirectly through your introductions. If you accept any fees from clients, always disclose that you will be receiving a share of the commissions from agents — you could, of course, point out that, but for this, your fees would be higher. If an agent ever attempts to deprive you of your share, do not give him a second chance. There are quite enough honest agents about, all clamouring for someone who will introduce new business.

Procedure to start business   Draft three separate letters to promote the service. Letter No. 1 should be sent to some fifty major UK companies, whose names can easily be found in the *Financial Times*. Try to find out the name of the managing director, or personnel director, and write to him personally, beginning along the following lines:

> *Dear Mr Smith*
> Overseas Executives
> *This service has been established specifically to assist UK personnel overseas who may, sooner or later, wish to return to this country.*
>
> *Our prime objective is to find ideal homes in parts of the UK best suited to the working or retirement requirements of each individual. We are confident*

that the time is right for serious consideration to be given to the matter, regardless of the actual date that the property will be required ... etc.

Letter No. 2, to be sent to estate agents, could be phrased as follows:

This company is entirely concerned with finding suitable homes for overseas clients returning to the UK.

We provide a highly efficient and confidential service and would be pleased to establish a mutually profitable working arrangement with your firm. If this is acceptable, we would propose to pass all enquiries concerning your area to you on the understanding that they would receive the prompt attention of a partner. On completion of business, we would look to you for 25 per cent of all gross fees and commissions that you receive in this connection ...

Letter No. 3 is your reply to answers to your advertisements, and should begin more or less as follows:

Thank you for your kind enquiry in answer to our recent advertisement in the Sunday Times.

This company specializes in assisting those planning to return to the UK to find suitable homes. We operate through a network of agents throughout the country which enables us to provide a unique and personal service ...

Points gathered during preliminary negotiations Personnel officers of five out of fifty companies interested in discussing the concept.

One bank prepared to grant 'loans-to-retirement' to own employees.

One company would consider possible advantages of harnessing idea to executive benefit scheme.

Consult firm of chartered accountants to discuss financial considerations of new business.

Estimate of initial cost of starting business   If your wife can type, fine. Otherwise, consider initially using a local agency and print service. Obtain quotations for headed stationery if you have decided to have a trade name.

Thoroughly check the likely cost of launching the business, bearing in mind that you may not receive any real fees for the first few months. It should be possible to make most telephone calls after lunch when it's cheaper. Allow an adequate amount for travelling; it is often a good investment to travel comfortably — do not economize on essentials: if you believe your profits will be seriously prejudiced by your spending an extra few pounds on taxis, you are definitely starting the wrong business. Ignoring the cost of your time, you would probably not need to spend £500 to know whether you are likely to get the business off the ground. Even if you have doubts, do not give up until you have re-assessed the operation several times to make quite sure that you are not missing something and that you are approaching the business the right way. For example, would the plan really only appeal to those over fifty? Would many expatriates prefer to retire to Spain where the weather is better and tax is lower? Even if you believe that you have got it right, re-examine every aspect of it regularly in an effort to make a good profitable service even better.

Conclusion You are now in business. You are in touch with different people who need your special expertise. You will also be earning money rather than sympathy. Finally, if the business works, still keep that notebook next to you to warehouse your new ideas.

Education

'Whom are you?' said he, for he had been to
night school.

George Ade

A young man named George Caprisou arrived in England
with one suit of clothing and £10. For eight years he worked
day and night in a small Soho restaurant in order to save
sufficient money to marry his old sweetheart and start his
own business. He bought a tiny bakery just off the motorway
to Hertford, and there introduced his speciality, raisin buns.
He had all his paper bags printed with the slogan, *Caprisou
Raisin Buns are the Finest in the World*; and he paid to
have, at either end of the little road, a sign carrying the same
message. The business prospered.

When George's son was born he took an oath that, unlike
his uneducated Greek father, the boy would have the finest
education that could be bought in England. He called the
lad Winston in the hope that such a name would encourage
him to excel in whatever he undertook. And so it was. In the
course of time the boy won a scholarship to read Economics
at Cambridge, and George was proud to give him a generous
allowance. Three years later, with a first-class degree, the
young man delighted his father by expressing a wish to join
him in business.

'You know, Father,' he confided, 'there is going to be a
recession and I think you should cut down expenses wherever possible. If it were my business, I would stop having
the bags printed and I would cancel the contracts for the
street signs.' Conscious of his son's degree, George listened
to the advice and followed the recommendations. Within
weeks he suffered a severe drop in turnover as fewer people
came to buy George's famous raisin buns.

'My son is brilliant,' George declared to a friend. 'Only a
month ago he was convinced we were heading for a recession and it's already arrived.'

THE
PROTECTION GAME

Insurance

Believers in the power of prayer still pay their
premiums.

Anon.

There is some evidence that it was the Phoenician and Baby-
lonian merchants who first practised devices which gave
them a degree of insurance protection; however, historians
in the field of international commerce consistently maintain
that modern insurance was first practised in Italy in the four-
teenth century. Initially, these contracts took the form of
contrived partnership agreements in order that the participants should not be accused of usury by the religious
leaders of their time. Pope Gregory IX (1145-1241) left no
margin for doubt that any man who entered into such a partnership would bring upon himself the 'perils of heaven'; and
more than three hundred years later, in 1586, Pope Sixtus V
was still condemning the use of insurance partnerships as a
pretext for usury. Shortly afterwards, the Church, despite
some objections, formally acknowledged that insurance
contracts were an explicit part of the commercial fabric.

Today, the term 'insurance' is interpreted to mean a contract under which one party, in consideration of the payment of a premium, undertakes to indemnify another party
against financial loss resulting from a specific risk. In terms

of protection, the vast majority of those living in Westernized civilizations have reason to be grateful to the insurance industry. But, as a moribund administrative jungle, it probably has no equal. In the UK the insurance company market is desperately in need of an innovator to drag it out of the nineteenth century and shake it out of the coma in which it has languished for so long. Men who — like Lee Iacocca of Chrysler or Arnold Weinstock of GEC — can turn failing companies into highly profitable major corporations, would quickly diagnose the sickness while others remain convinced that the patient is still alive and well.

To Mr Average, the prime purpose of the insurance world is to provide protection, on competitive terms, to private individuals, industry and commerce. In return, the insurer receives a premium which is carefully calculated to cover the risk involved, the overheads of the company and the dividend to shareholders, plus a reasonable margin for waste, inefficiency and negligence. The last three have become so much part of the fabric that no one would ever think of including them in the balance sheet.

In the following pages we shall examine the part which the law of WIN (waste, inefficiency and negligence) plays in the company world of insurance, risk and profit. For convenience' sake, WIN will also represent mis-information, miscalculation, stagnation and lack of imagination. They are all part of the same system.

The Fear Mongers

Only efficiency can produce losses for an
industry built on dread.

Amos Hargraves Jnr

Contrary to popular belief, and that of a large number of
insurance officials, the insurance industry is really in the
money business. The risk aspect of its operations is often
almost incidental as far as much of its business is concerned.
The art of recycling money is what generates the profit and
the real growth in the shares of insurance companies. Thus
it is not uncommon to find that an insurance company with
a premium income of £300,000,000 will produce an underwriting loss of £30,000,000 but an overall profit of, say,
£50,000,000. This latter figure is achieved from the wisely
conservative investment of premiums and reserves. With the
exception of Acts of God, such as hurricanes, avalanches
and volcanic eruptions, many everyday risks can be assessed
and adequately protected. For example, of the near five
million scheduled flights made in and from America in a
given year, less than five people died in aviation accidents.
On this basis it was a cinch for an insurance company to
offer American Express bargain rates for its card-holders.
With a million-to-one chance, the company only had to
make its calculations on the basis of 250,000-to-one to make it
sound interesting to everyone. This situation begs two
questions: first, how insurers justify charging five times that
amount to other healthy individuals on the same flight; and,
second, why American Express needs to be bothered with
an insurer. A risk with such odds could well be taken by a
corporation of that size without any anxiety. All it has to do
is to build a safety net in the form of re-insurance protection
should claims ever exceed a million. At $3 a head per flight,
American Express are collecting a lot of premium. Maybe
they are slightly biased as they own the insurance company
in question and there might be a certain amount of back

scratching. But, according to insurance figures, of every £1,000,000 collected in aviation personal-accident premiums, it is unlikely that more than £100,000 will be paid out. By any normal standard that does leave a margin for commission, expenses, errors or catastrophe. Of course, to create a real picture it is only necessary to make one's calculations on the substantially higher premiums charged to a larger number of individual air passengers who do not hold American Express cards. Bearing in mind that the odds on having an accident remain fairly constant, this should be printing money with a vengeance. For those who are curious, there are no commissions and no overheads when companies like American Express effect master policies. The premium is simply added to the price of the air ticket.

Not every area of risk is quite as easy to assess, and statistics are not consistently reliable; shrewd re-insurance programmes and good management however, can, in reducing the risk of enormous losses, take the sting out of most of the suffering in a bad underwriting year. Nevertheless, screams of distress emerge from the trapdoors of domestic-fire underwriters as they bemoan their losses arising from increased claims. These are the lamentations of honest men fighting against intensive competition, in a claims-ridden society, to earn a modest percentage from their labours. Yet in their distress they forget to mention that for years they have paid commissions up to 50 per cent to building societies (who introduce a very substantial business to them) as against the normal rate of 15 per cent to their brokers and agents. This is despite the fact that the latter group relieve them of a fair amount of their administration costs. So here we have insurance companies paying up to 50 per cent to privileged agents. This, allowing for administrative overheads, leaves a maximum of 20 per cent for claims at a time when fire hazards are creating havoc with premiums. Instead of adjusting the commission terms, insurers plead with their assessors to adopt a tougher line with claims. This is a symptom of WIN's Law. It would also be reasonable to assume that hundreds of thousands of house-owners insured through the master policies of building societies have not got the remotest idea of their real protection: few would realize, for instance, that there is often no cover for alternative accommodation, in the event of a serious fire, under their property insurance. Normally, for some strange reason, this item is insured as a percentage of the contents insurance: in the London area this compensation would be unlikely to cover the cost of alternative accommodation for more than six weeks. If this cover were related to the building costs, it would make a great deal more sense. In the meantime, there are probably several million people who are inadequately insured. The 50 per cent commission they receive from the underwriters does not require the building societies to make such facts known to their clients.

But things are not always as bad as this. Sometimes they are worse. Burglary is a growth industry, they say, and every insurance clerk repeats: 'Burglary is a growth industry'. This means that not only are the burglars getting richer, but so are the assessors, the burglar alarm installers and the large collection of retailers who make a business out of replacing stolen goods at inflated prices. Insurers continue to increase premiums and demand that extra locks, stronger window frames, touch-sensitive glass, and better safes be installed. And, at the same time, the number of claims continues to rise, the number of arrests remains constant – and, insurers convincingly intone, 'Burglary is a growth business.' Nobody considers the 10-15 per cent discount which all insurers obtain from jewellers, furriers and others replacing stolen goods. On this basis it could be argued that the real rate for burglary and all-risks insurance is really 10-15 per cent higher than that declared – there would appear to be no legal obligation for insurers to make this disclosure.

There is no complete answer to the burglary problem which is exacerbated by unemployment and ineffective sentences. The fact remains, however, that there would be substantially fewer burglaries if there were fewer fences. The professional burglar is not interested in hanging on to his spoils: his job is to know the property, assess its contents from the lifestyle of its occupants, and complete the job within five minutes flat. After that his only interest is to off-load the stolen goods and happily accept up to 20 per cent of their value – it is the fence who makes the real money.

Considering the huge sums paid out each year in burglary claims, one wonders why insurance companies have not clubbed together to finance a small group of private detectives to track down the fences. Instead, they content themselves with offering rewards of 10 per cent of the claim for information leading to the recovery of the goods; sometimes this works but, more often than not, loyalty within the burglary profession overcomes temptation. The time is long overdue for underwriters to realize that the rules of the game have changed: high premiums will make the business profitable, and ingenious locking systems will not deter the resolute burglar. Top operators in the crime business are familiar with the rules, the risks and the rewards. They know only too well that unless they can off-load quickly, they are out of business. The police know it too but in many ways their hands are tied when it comes to adopting an innovative approach to crime. There is really no group better placed to help society and themselves than the major insurance companies. They also have the means, the experience and the connections to make it worthwhile for those, such as informers, prepared to co-operate.

There are simpler innovations that might be made in the insurance world. It is legendary that when Lord Marks, the chairman of Marks & Spencer, cancelled the use of all inter-departmental memos, the company saved 6,000,000 pieces of paper a year. If members of the British Insurance Association saved only one piece of paper per motor vehicle insured, the saving could well be ten times that figure; a streamlining of the renewal system would probably save a similar amount. The reason why such simple steps are not implemented is probably connected with the reason why an industry with such a vast number of employees has shown itself incapable of reducing overheads by a mere 10 per cent. This position could change overnight if branch managers and other senior staff were offered bonuses for achievement rather than acquiescence. The saving in labour, materials, printing and postage, which would arise from a real document-economy drive could produce millions of pounds of profit for the industry. It might also create more efficient staff.

At the deeper end, another student of WIN's Law might ask why an industry with declared long-term funds in excess of £100,000,000,000 and a steady annual cashflow of £14,000,000,000, should not have established its own direct or indirect banking interest. A mere tenth of one per cent (0.01 per cent) improvement in performances would produce an additional annual income of £100,000,000 for the 400 BIA members. Seeing that this financial muscle is greater than that of our largest bank, the National Westminster, one can understand the curiosity of the student of WIN's Law. Even if the system would prevent any benefit accruing to policyholders, at least the shareholders would benefit. It is the ability to recognize and exploit opportunities to squeeze additional percentages that has enabled American banks like Manufacturers Hanover to break into some of Britain's largest industrial accounts. The great day of reckoning in the insurance industry must surely be on the way.

In the meantime it is important to understand the methods used to market insurance and, more particularly, the role played by the various classes of insurance broker.

The Middle Men

Insurance agents are those who earn their
livelihoods introducing superstitious clients to
optimistic underwriters.

Anon.

In simplest terms, an insurance broker is an independent
intermediary for more than one insurer. His function is to
provide unbiased advice to clients in relation to policies
which he or they feel should be effected. It is somewhat
incongruous that, while acting in the interest of their clients,
these brokers are remunerated by insurance companies and
underwriters. In practice, however, the system has worked
remarkably well, and the majority of professional brokers
have not been unduly influenced by variations in commission structures. Most recognize that, in a competitive world,
to offer the best advice, on the most favourable terms, to
their clients is a long-term investment. Broadly, insurance
brokers fall into the following four categories:

Lloyd's Brokers. These are authorized to place business
with underwriters at Lloyd's and invariably hold agencies
with most of the major insurance companies. They are
obliged by Lloyd's to have a high standard of qualification
and experience, and their financial standing and code of
behaviour is regularly monitored by Lloyd's itself. Their scale
of commissions is unified and no underwriter would consider offering preferential terms to different brokers. Each
member of a firm of Lloyd's brokers wishing to be admitted
to the underwriting room has to submit an individual application for approval. Each application is vetted very carefully,
and acceptance is dependent on the applicant's background,
qualification and, in the case of younger people, supervision.
This is no mere formality, for the Committee of Lloyd's is
very concerned about who should be approved. Once
accepted, each individual, or his firm, is obliged to pay a
substantial annual fee for the privilege. Furthermore, a

special department at Lloyd's inspects the annual balance sheet of every firm of Lloyd's brokers to ensure the adequacy of their funds for the business which they are handling. Of the £4,000,000,000 of foreign premium coming to Lloyd's each year, the vast majority is dealt with by the top twenty firms of Lloyd's brokers. These firms are geared to handle the larger commercial and industrial accounts and employ thousands of highly qualified staff, many of them numbering among the most skilled and highly paid in the City.

Outside Brokers. The term simply implies that this group are not Lloyd's brokers. They represent insurance compan- ies, and when they wish to place business in Lloyd's, they use the services of a Lloyd's broker. Many are well qualified academically, but they tend to act mostly for domestic clients, avoiding the high overheads of handling many classes of overseas business. Most established outside brokers have built their businesses by providing a more personal service to private clients than do their Lloyd's colleagues. Although often well able to cope with most classes of business, it is unlikely that a major oil or shipping group would place its business with non-Lloyd's brokers. This is not a reflection on ability or integrity; it is just that people dealing with vast risks and premiums prefer to deal where there is most muscle. Unfortunately, but understand- ably, a certain number of outside brokers have tended to be influenced by commission terms when recommending policies. Lack of commission control has been a very definite flaw in the industry. Apart from influencing advice and clouding the good judgement of many fringe brokers, it was largely responsible for insurance company failures in the seventies.

Although the inexperienced broker has come- in for a great deal of attack over the years, the real culprits are the insurance companies. It is they and they alone who allow people to sell insurance to the public regardless of expertise or knowledge. At one time it was far easier to get insurance agencies than a licence to sell Coca-Cola. Major insurance companies happily threw ethics and business standards to the wind and indiscriminately created competition for their loyal brokers. Pounding the streets of large and small towns, insurance company inspectors hawked their agencies to garage mechanics, bank clerks, landscape gardeners, plumbers, undertakers, dress manufacturers, estate agents, decorators and anyone who was prepared to listen to stories of easy money. The position is not much improved, in spite of limited safeguards that have more recently been introduced. It is against this background that certain commission-hungry brokers should be judged. In the world of jungle warfare, insurance companies have little to learn. Most of the problems in the agency system are of their making, and their loyalties to bona-fide brokers have often proved as steadfast as ping-pong balls in a thunderstorm.

Life Insurance Brokers. These are specialists in the field of life insurance, most of whom started as agents for one or another of the better known life offices and then went on to develop their own practices as independent operators. This enables them to provide the best policies on the market rather than be restricted to the contracts of an individual company. Life-insurance brokers endeavour to specialise but in fact tend to offer a broadly based service in the area of financial planning and often include pensions, mortgages and loan negotiations among their packages. A number of highly qualified experts operate in this field but, here again, the agency system leaves the door wide open to the un-informed and the less scrupulous. As a rough guide, a good life-insurance broker is not a dabbler. He knows his business, his market and his competition, and he is happy to discuss them all with his clients. Again, he is paid by the insurers — most of whom are happy to double-cross him by encouraging and creating competition to his business.

Fringe Brokers. These are a miscellaneous group of mixed occupations who carry insurance agencies for the benefit of their own business, for their friends or as a sideline. In academic terms they are mostly out of their depth, and their lack of knowledge is matched only by their inexperience. At best, they do little harm as they are often acting for the largest insurers in the country — those who most favour the system but will always meet legitimate claims. At worst, the policies they sell may well be inappropriate, excessive, or, where they are guided by innocence or ignorance, grossly inadequate. Blindly following the belief that 'one policy is like another', this band of insurance operators introduce their naive clients to companies who reward them with the same commission terms enjoyed by reputable professional brokers. Uninhibited by training and unburdened by expertise, these part-time business producers are anathema to the professional insurance world and a poor reflection on those insurance companies who support them. It is only surprising that professional insurance brokers have not banded together to put pressure on the leading insurance companies who perpetuate the system. How strange it is that those with so much buying power are happy to continue to feed those companies that do so little to enhance the image of the industry. The story is told of an eminent lawyer who once attended a conference of senior insurance company officials. He was particularly keen to meet the one representative of the broking fraternity. 'How will I recognize him?' he asked. 'You can't miss him,' was the response. 'He'll be the one with the knives in his back.'

In practical terms it would make sense for the fringe agent to be outlawed and instead permitted to act as an intermediary for registered brokers. At least, in this way Mr Public would stand a good chance of receiving sound independent advice and fair value.

For the layman, and even for the busy professional, the insurance broker should be included in the panel of financial advisers consulted to provide both security and protection. Insurance broking is no longer the business for the amateur. There is also little to be gained by dealing with insurers direct except the knowledge that the companies will pocket the commission which would otherwise be paid to the qualified independent broker. Those who choose to patronize fringe agents should ask themselves if they would consult a DIY brain surgeon or retain an untrained housebuilder.

Motor Insurance – What a Hoot

Don't be so sure that your lawyer is as
crooked as he's supposed to be.

Anon.

There was once a market trader who swore that he sold his
wares for less than cost. When challenged to explain why he
bothered, he answered, 'It's my business, that's why.'

The same argument could often be made for the motor-
insurance industry. In the case of the trader, everybody
knows that his declaration is part of his selling technique.
This is not so for motor insurers. Most of them started off by
being unimaginative; then euphoria set in and they
developed tunnel vision. Later, inspired by mental inactivity,
they graduated to a state of paralysed thinking. Innovation is
a foreign word in the motor-insurance world, where the skill
of the average underwriter is measured by the amount of
paper he generates. Despite the ability of several hundred
motor insurers to generate premiums of nearly
£4,000,000,000 they still manage to produce an annual loss
of £349,000,000. Like well-trained choristers, the underwriters repeat their old refrain, 'Claims costs have risen';
comforted by the silent response, they continue to underwrite poor-quality business in high-risk areas in the pious
hope that increased death on the roads will eventually
reduce the number of careless drivers. If there is another
reason, it is difficult to discern.

It is therefore not surprising that knowledgeable people
have been crying out for years for motor insurers to put their
houses in order. It is only amazing that so little has been
done about it. The man in the street and even his better
versed brother would be shattered to learn exactly how in-
efficient and moribund a large part of this industry is.

To begin with, one only has to examine the agency
system. Some of our largest insurers are happy to grant
motor insurance agencies to any garage or motor dealer.

After all, they argue, these are the people best placed to get the business. This is often true. No one is readier to buy insurance from a dealer than the innocent, the irresponsible, or the young and over-enthusiastic, who, having just bought a car from the dealer, is all too eager to get it on the road. The fact that the motor-trading industry enjoys the same reputation as the old-time horse-traders and that the average dealer is likely to know more about Greek philosophy than he does about insurance, doesn't seem to occur to anyone. The individual receives a policy which he doesn't understand and the insurance company is happy to pay the dealer the same commission as is paid to qualified brokers. As, however, there is no broker involved, the company itself deals with all queries and claims — multiplied a million times, this adds a useful item to overheads. It doesn't stop there.

The motor dealer not only gets a commission, but he is given at least one month's credit, even though everyone knows that he doesn't have to give any. In practice, he doesn't take a month's credit — he takes two. Furthermore, he continues to enjoy commission for as long as the car buyer renews his policy or effects any other policy with the same insurer. With his ignorance tempered by high-pressure selling, the motor trader is a good business producer. The fact that it is estimated to cost the insurance industry fifty per cent more than business received through the qualified intermediary, does not appear to strike the motor insurers as important. Motor underwriters still have confidence in the system and in their hymn books. Each year the chorus gets louder and no one complains about the cacophony. But it doesn't stop there.

In gratitude for being placed in a position to build up a profitable sideline without knowledge or overheads, how does the motor industry reciprocate? It takes every opportunity to inflate the cost of any insured claim that arrives at its garages. There cannot be a car owner who has not been asked if he has an insurance claim when he has driven his battered vehicle in for repair. Of course, the motor insurer has got assessors who struggle to do a good job, but in practice this means that, when possible, they get a £300 claim down to £250, knowing all the while that the garage should not be charging more than £200.

There are a number of actions which could be taken to improve this unsatisfactory position. In the first place, insurance agencies should be withdrawn from all unqualified intermediaries; if necessary, government legislation could be introduced to bring this about. In the second place — and this could have more far-reaching effects — garages should be insurance-approved. On this basis, any garage that obviously inflates a claim would be automatically reported to a central insurance intelligence unit; on doing so a second time, they would be struck off for a year, and, the third time, permanently. There can be no doubt that this would not only create a healthier and more efficient industry, but would be bound eventually to bring about reductions in premiums. When this principle was submitted to a major UK insurer as long ago as 1955, he answered, 'That would be disloyal to some of our long-standing agents.' The response made as much sense than as it does today.

In assessing risks in the motor industry, it seems strange that no insurer has attempted to write policies at premium rates related to mileage. Statistics show that the chances of an accident rise steadily with the number of miles driven by Mr or Mrs Average in each given geographical area. It is estimated that Mr X, aged forty-two, has 2.6 times more chance of having an accident on his ten-mile drive to work each day, than Mrs X, aged sixty-eight, who uses exactly the same model of car to drive to church once a week. Yet, often, the premiums are identical. A relatively simple way of collecting premiums would be to add an insurance tax to the price of petrol. It could well become a government-oriented exercise to be managed by the insurance industry. The fringe benefits offered by individual insurers would maintain a competitive element in the business. The resultant reduction in insurance staff, and in paper, printing and postage could put motor insurance among the high earners. The only real uncertainty is whether an industry that produces a turnover of around £4,000,000,000 could generate enough co-operation among its members.

Another area where reform is long overdue is in the actual

settlement of claims. Insurance attitudes here oscillate between the ridiculous and the confused, with inconsistency substituted for flexibility. The treatment of claims for personal injury tend to provide more material benefits for the legal profession than for either the claimants or the insurance companies. When an insurer retains the best lawyer in town, his instructions are to get the claim settled as quickly as possible on the most disadvantageous terms to the client, or at least to find all the precedents in the records to minimize the settlement. This of course prolongs the agony. The provoked insured employs his own lawyer with instructions to make the most of the meal. In no time at all, integrity takes on the form of elastic, and the meters in the lawyer's offices start working overtime. At the end of the day, the insurers invariably pay more than they might have done if they had made a respectable offer in the first place. Anyone doubting this should study the number of motor claims that are actually settled at the door of the court-room.

What is difficult to understand is why a man earning £2,000 a month will be grateful to employers who continue to pay him while he recovers from falling over his lawn-mower, and yet feels entitled to sue for a fortune if he suffers identical injury in a motor accident. Surely it is not beyond the ability of the industry to obtain government blessings for at least a limited schedule of compensations to be agreed? As an example, a person expected to recover fully from a relatively minor accident, like a broken arm, would receive 120 per cent of his salary plus reasonable expenses. The client would know exactly where he stood, the insurers would make more profit and the lawyers would have to adjust their meters. A fabulous illustration of the philosophy of contingency lawyers was given in a film starring Walter Matthau as a claim-fixing lawyer. 'The motor accident has caused you to suffer a spinal injury and it's likely that you will never again be able to use your left leg or most of the fingers on your right hand,' he tells his young client.

'You're mad,' says the client, 'I can move all my limbs perfectly well.'

'Of course you can,' replies the lawyer, 'if you want to blow a million bucks.'

There may well be more than an element of truth in the script but, then, claims are handled differently in the States. In this country, with the exception of more serious claims and injuries, the principle of agreed compensation could be implemented in many instances. The main problem would probably be getting the insurance companies to agree among themselves.

Early Call

A solicitor arrived at the Holy Gates requesting an immediate opportunity to express an important grievance. When the angel in charge of complaints granted him an interview, he exploded: 'I'm only fifty-four. I had a very successful practice. I was at the height of my career. None of my friends have been called at my age, so why did you have to pick on me?'

'I'll look into it immediately,' answered the angel. Within a short while he returned smiling to the solicitor.

'Your records appear to be in order,' he stated. 'According to the copies of your time-sheets we calculate that you must be at least eighty-nine.'

Protecting the Innocents

Ignorance of the law does not prevent the
losing lawyer from collecting his fees.

Anon.

Third-party insurance cover provides protection against
being held responsible for injury to individuals or damage to
property. It follows that premiums must vary according to
the occupation of the insured and the materials or machinery over which he has direct or indirect control. Thus a
building contractor erecting a twenty-storey building, or the
manufacturer of explosives, would expect to be charged
many times the premium charged to an advertising agent,
the chances of the latter being responsible for a serious accident being relatively remote.

Claims in this area offer the maximum scope for imaginative and conniving solicitors; experience, no doubt,
prompted an old wit to define a jury as twelve honest men
with the task of deciding which party has the better lawyer
— words supported by the enormous variation in damages
for apparently identical claims. It strikes many as unacceptable that an affluent sportsman who effects accident cover
for £50,000 against the possibility of losing a leg, will nevertheless try to claim ten times that figure from a third party
should a claim arise. How learned judges are frequently
convinced that such claims are valid remains a mystery.

In 1981, the parents of a four-year-old boy were killed in a
air crash in California. The father had been a lorry driver
earning the equivalent of £120 a week. Had he lived, his
salary might well have doubled during his working life,
assuming that he had remained in permanent employment.
If, on this basis, we assume that he might have been happy
to support his son until the boy reached the age of twenty-
one, a sum approaching £75,000 would have been generous
compensation; however, allowing a sensible item for pain
and suffering — which can never be calculated in such cases

— the figure might be raised to £100,000. In the event the American judge awarded damages of £1,000,000 — a third of which compensated the lawyers for their time.

The ease with which unwarranted compensation of this magnitude is enjoyed must surely encourage many to mis-represent their suffering when real or imaginary injuries are sustained. This widespread approach to personal third-party claims enables lawyers with fertile minds and few ethics to take insurers to the cleaners. The story of the New York lawyer who, having listened sympathetically to a client explain how he had had a bad fall outside a small store in Fifth Avenue, suddenly raised his hands above his head and asked, 'Even with your injuries, couldn't you have dragged yourself another twenty feet to Macy's?' may just contain a grain of truth. In 1977, a Gallup poll in America showed that only 26 per cent of those questioned believed that lawyers maintained a high standard of honesty. An editor of the American *Lawyer* magazine decided to put this to the test and, choosing twelve attorneys at random, she told each one the identical story: 'I stepped off the curb in the vicinity of some construction work, and I fell over and injured my back.'

Each time, she meticulously emphasized that she was some way from the actual building work but was willing to 'shift' the location if it helped. Four lawyers assured her she had no case against anybody. All the others, except one, told her to shift the scene of the accident *slightly* and sue hell out of the construction company. The odd lawyer offered to take the case for the customary 30 per cent share of awards but added, 'Basically, I'll help you but you've got to ask yourself honestly if you're up to the strain of lying at that level.'

In England, no one is quite sure whether it is a question of attitude or temperament that prevents judges from taking the same jaundiced view on compensation as their American colleagues. Whichever it is, it would be a very sad day for all but the lawyers if award-sharing was introduced into the British legal system. The truth is that it is probably the insur-ance companies themselves, and their attempts to avoid settling claims fairly, that have created so many dishonest claimants and bent lawyers.

Paying for the Trip

Fear encourages caution, prayers and insurance.

Amos Hargraves Jnr

In the days when crime was still in its infancy, before even burglary became a growth industry, there were institutions, splendidly misnamed, known as Friendly Societies.

These were the benevolent organizations that encouraged the poor to make provision for funeral expenses and other disbursements which Providence might unexpectedly ordain; the feeble and the indigent would thus be prepared for the financial overheads incurred in joining their Maker, or the costs arising from His acts or their carelessness. With ingenuity disguised as benevolence, some of the institutions proceeded to provide a measure of security and comfort for the unfortunate, proud and often unwary masses. Invariably housed in dingy offices, some of the promotors and principals convincingly projected images of frugality which enabled them to fleece their impecunious clients with all humility.

With the benefit of hindsight, it is not surprising that among those operating these ancient orders should be some seeking their portion of this lucrative market. Quick to recognize the difficulty in infiltrating the ranks of the establishment, they drafted their own unique policies. With a shrewd assessment of the vast potential available, the contracts were carefully drafted for those with insufficient time or education to understand them. Thus were created some of the most imaginative and confusing insurance documents ever sold. Unlike the large institutions, which were simply determined to make exorbitant profits, these little centres of trust and hope were printing money. The letter of the law was always observed — but the spirit of the law was a luxury that few could afford.

The Friendly Societies, however, never pretended to be in

or cater for the jet class. The following are typical of the benefits provided in the good old days of this century and even today in some cities.

Loss of life	£100
Loss of limb	£100
Loss of one leg and one arm	£200
Loss of one finger or one eye	£ 50
Loss of two fingers	£ 75
Loss of two eyes	£100

Such policies guaranteed treble benefits if claims arose through accidents involving aircraft, military vehicles or trains. This had nothing to do with benevolence, but was simply because the insurers could easily recover such costs from the carriers. The small print in the policies always gave the insurers such rights. In any case, in those days less than one in five hundred thousand working people ever saw the inside of a plane. War risks were invariably excluded. The cost of each unit of cover was around two pence a week — an apparently modest premium which in reality was at least five times as expensive as policies issued by the major insurance companies. It was the weekly door-to-door method of collection that sold the policies to the budget-minded in the poverty-striken industrial cities. Variations on the type of cover were endless but records of actual claims are often difficult to come by.

The Friendly Societies, having by the twentieth century grown rather less than benevolent, were probably at their peak during the 1940s. Since then, many have folded, while those that exist sell the more formal types of policies.

Today's more orthodox, competitive kind of accident policy for a fit man under sixty, with a non-hazardous occupation, provides protection of £10,000 for an annual premium of about £10. In real terms, it is doubtful if insurers pay out more than 15-20 per cent of their premiums in actual claims, but such expenses as commissions, administrative costs and head-office overheads manage to produce relatively modest profit figures. If it were not for the Post Office's record of incompetence and poor management, one could imagine the vast network of post offices as ideally placed to issue standard personal accident policies at half current market price. With most of its overheads already covered, the Post Office should still be able to make a very useful profit.

Alternatively, an enterprising group of garages or super-markets might well entertain the idea of issuing their own policies, virtually carrying the risks themselves. Instead of giving away Hong Kong-made watches or Taiwan tumblers, petrol stations could link personal accident protection to petrol sales. Similarly, supermarkets might give, say, a week's free cover to each customer who spent over £X. A sensible re-insurance programme would enable them to restrict their maximum aggregate loss and still enjoy a profit plus all the benefits of a first-class PR exercise. They might make more sales, too.

Money or Your Life

Pure life insurance guarantees your heirs your
money to enjoy without your reproaches.
Amos Hargraves Jnr

Ignoring pensions, annuities and investment bonds, life-insurance policies are divided into three types of contracts:

1   Whole-life policies, which demand premiums to be paid throughout life or, more often, up to the age of seventy-five.
2   Term insurance, which provides protection for a given number of years.
3   Endowment insurance, which provides protection and a guaranteed sum at the end of ten or more years.

Each of these contracts can be tailored to meet specific requirements but the individual principles behind them remain the same. These are the policies which, in the UK, produce in aggregate over £1,250,000,000 in new sums insured every year. In America, where there are alleged to be over 250,000 full-time life-insurance agents, the figures are much higher — but the high-pressure selling techniques of that nation are reflected in the fact that in the early eighties over 20 per cent of all policies lapsed within the first two years. On the other hand, Americans tend to be far more conscious of illnesses, phobias and statistics than Europeans. Typically, US life-assurance salesmen would point out the grim fact that 30 per cent of deaths among married men under the age of forty-four are caused by cancer; they do not mention that 64 per cent die in accidents and that the total number of deaths in that age group, from all causes, is about 220,000, out of a population of 200,000,000. Quoting a figure like 0.3 per cent is not exactly a sales-aid when it comes to selling life insurance.

Zealously applying pressure on the human buttons of hope and fear has enabled life-insurance companies to operate successfully for nearly three hundred years. Throughout this period, countless widows and orphans have been able to survive their tragedies with dignity and a degree of comfort. There is no other industry in the world that can claim to have consistently provided security and protection for hundreds of thousands of people in every section of society. But the fact remains that life insurance is sold rather than bought, and the business-generating methods employed over the years could fill textbooks for confidence tricksters.

These practices have been around so long that, having had integrity grafted onto their reputations, they now enjoy places of honour in the insurance jungle. Our major insurance companies continued to perpetuate such sales philosophies, on which the success of their ancestors was built up. These, known as industrial life offices, simply because they used to operate largely in industrial areas, provided a door-to-door service among the poorer classes. Apart from having to budget and scrape to find their own miserable premiums, countless were often persuaded to effect similar policies on the lives of their little children. This was in the days when, having reached the age of five, a child had a life expectancy of sixty-five years. On this basis the door-to-door premiums frequently came to cost them twenty times as much as they would have had to pay a reputable company charging annual premiums.

Another indefensible practice was peculiarly British and largely the creation of the non-industrial life-insurance companies. In an effort to spread the gospel of security and perpetuate an analogy between longevity tables and roulette, the majority of the larger life companies structured their agency systems with the enthusiasm and discrimination of ice-cream vendors. The high levels of commission and ignorance enjoyed by most of their unqualified and in-experienced representatives virtually guaranteed that large numbers of policyholders would get poor value for their money. Mesmerized by the fear of sudden death or becoming uninsurable, most members of the unsuspecting public accepted quotations in a hurry without checking the competition. Like the single rifleman with only one bullet facing a line of twenty men, many life-insurance salesmen perfected an ability to induce instant firing-squad paranoia. In pure commercial terms this gift is considered more valuable than any education.

Against this background the life-insurance industry has grown to become one of the largest employers in the world of free enterprise, and a major power in the money markets of every capital. With more information and greater expertise more readily available to the man in the street, and more and more people recognizing the role of the independent broker, life-insurance companies have been obliged to provide better value and more facts and figures. Furthermore, there have, since the early 1980s, been distinct signs that many are making genuine attempts to put their agency systems on a more professional basis. It is no longer so easy for people such as garage mechanics, travel agents, gown merchants, plumbers and estate agents to obtain agencies from reputable life-insurance companies.

When the pound was worth its name and premiums qualified for tax relief, life insurance ran neck and neck with religion in providing comfort to the masses. Thanks to a succession of politically inspired economists, the pound has plummeted in value, tax loopholes have been plugged and fewer and fewer people see prayer as a negotiable commodity. The halcyon days are over and life companies have rushed to expand their interests into pension business, unit trusts and mortgages. With the enthusiasm of the convert, many are now genuinely determined to show their policyholders the regard previously reserved for management and shareholders. They are all too well aware that aggressive competition from other investment managers will make many realize that term insurance can often be a far better buy than either whole-life or endowment. Competent managers of private pension funds have long recognized that little is to be achieved by confusing *death* insurance with fund management. With the loss of the 17 per cent tax relief previously allowed on life premiums, more intelligent people must be expected to reach the same conclusion. The following table, though not precise, serves to indicate the figures which influence the premium calculations of actuaries:

Of 1,000 people aged:	*This number may be expected to die this year:*
20	1.4
30	1.4
40	2.4
50	6.0
55	9.5

It is important to remember that the figures relate to numbers per thousand — so that under 1 per cent of the average 1,000 between the ages of fifty and fifty-five will die this year. Another significant figure is that over 55 per cent of people will live to celebrate their seventy-fifth birthdays. This means that, on balance, insurance companies will be able to hold their interest-earning life premiums longer, the government will have to pay pensions longer and more people will have to wait for middle age before they inherit.

There are still far too many people who arrange whole-life policies, which are ideal for long-term protection, when all they need is term insurance. A typical example would be a thirty-five-year-old father who wants to buy insurance to ensure that, in the event of his death in the next ten years, £20,000 will be available to cover school fees. Many agents in such a case have been known to recommend a whole-life policy, requiring an annual premium of about £240, when all that is necessary is a ten-year term insurance costing £36. Furthermore a term contract provides the right, for just another £8 a year, to buy whole-life insurance, up to £20,000, at any time during the ten-year period at normal rates of premium without any additional medical evidence. It is worth mentioning that the whole-life policy would earn the agent about £400 in commission and the term contract about £8. It would be quite unfair to blame all the wheeler-dealers who have enjoyed the perks provided so readily by leaders in the industry. They make no claim to be financial advisers or qualified insurance brokers, they are simply honest, commission-hungry hawkers who had the wit to get onto a profitable bandwagon. With differences in commission often amounting to many hundreds of pounds per policy, few part-time agents have experienced difficulty in deciding which policy to sell. Leading insurance companies who appointed these jokers as agents accept no responsibility, adopting the attitude that man is emancipated and, over the age of eighteen, can look after himself. This system is however in the process of being overhauled and efforts are being made to cut such agents out.

Endowment insurance is quite another matter. Although the unfortunate agency system has been just as rampant, there was less chance of people getting a poor deal. Companies like Scottish Widows, The Friends Provident and a dozen or more others have consistently been more discerning and have long produced first-class policies with bonuses which, over many years, have made them secure, attractive investments. The major disadvantage of an endowment policy, as opposed to putting your money into building societies or certain investment trusts, is that the money is tied up for a given number of years. Any demand for cash before maturity invariably demands a substantial discount; and any loan taken against the security of the policy requires interest to be paid. This means that the insured has to accept a loss if he wishes to redeem some of his own money or pay interest to borrow it. It must be seen as no mean achievement for an industry successfully to persuade the public, for nearly three hundred years, that this is an equitable arrangement. The time must be long overdue for an enterprising life-insurance company to offer an endowment policy which provides continuity of full cover if part or all of the policy were surrendered. This would mean that a modest additional annual premium could provide emergency life protection should a policyholder need his own money before the expiry date of the policy.

The genuine peace of mind and comfort which life insurance has brought to millions cannot be exaggerated. Furthermore, in the field of under-average lives, insurance companies often play a rarely considered role of life lengthener: suddenly faced with dire warnings from the insurers' medical examiners and with ominously loaded premiums, thousands of the over-stressed or overweight have changed their lifestyles for the better.

In 1965, a small group under the chairmanship of Air Vice-Marshal Stanbridge, a retired deputy chief of the RAF Medical Services, decided to investigate the medical intelligence which influenced life-insurance ratings. They recruited Dr Berwick Wright, then head of medical services for BUPA, and the chief medical officer of the Equitable Life Assurance Company of New York (which employed more full-time medical and research staff than the top twenty British life offices put together). Two years later the findings of this little group convinced several insurance companies that, with the advances made in medical science, a more enlightened attitude could be adopted towards certain health categories, and, accordingly, their premiums rated more lightly. Armed with this information, several professional life brokers were confident that they could make an enormous impact on the £480,000,000 of business underwritten for second- and third-class lives. It was a reasonable assumption but the well-advertised savings which could be enjoyed attracted little response. The exercise had failed. It took nearly twenty years for the answer to reveal itself.

In the 1980s, another enterprising life-insurance company suddenly realized the potential business which under-average lives could provide. Ignoring the progress in medical science, they conducted their own market research and then produced a new policy at substantially higher rates than usual. The proposal form contained only five questions; if they were answered satisfactorily, no medical examination was required and a policy was issued. It was a normal policy, on terms applicable to *first-class* lives, without any mention of premium loadings or special conditions. That was the answer. The policyholders accepted the higher premiums without comparing them with those of other companies: what they wanted were policies that still described them as being in good health. The scheme was an immediate success, and the company continues to find the business very profitable.

The life-insurance industry is probably in a healthier state today than it has ever been. It is putting its house in order by taking more care over the presentation of its products and those who represent them. It has been shaken by changes in the tax system, the mass enthusiasm for unit trust investments, and, in no small way, by one man. In 1962, a young South African lawyer, Mark Weinberg, arrived in Britain and started a small life-insurance company with £50,000. He brought a new dimension to the industry, for, as well as being an innovative thinker, he explained to people exactly what he was selling them and precisely what they could expect for their money. Later, he pioneered the managed pension bond which was simply a share-portfolio investment approved by the Inland Revenue. In less than twenty years, he made several million pounds for himself and his colleagues, and he virtually put the British life-insurance industry on its toes. His success is well earned, his reputation is unique, and — strangely, in a world where achievement is often met with suspicion — he enjoys the admiration and respect of his peers.

With changing demands and attitudes, with larger pensions and more knowledgeable thinking, there are likely to be further changes in the life-insurance industry. It will certainly continue to serve the community but its products could well be marketed differently. There will be fewer part-time fringe agents and more professional brokers, but there could also be a new class of intermediary — not the dabbler in search of a sideline but the marketing expert. As with personal accident insurance, enterprising retailers might consider selling insurance. It is not difficult to envisage an enterprising oil company supplying 'Petrol Life' policies, with every ten gallons of petrol buying one week's cover. On the same principle we might have 'Tesco Life' or 'Marks & Spencer Life'. It would not require a genius to design attractive policies with adequate safeguards. The interest on the premiums, let alone the profit margins, could make such exercises worthwhile to the pioneers; and it could sound the knell to many door-to-door agents and those who employ them. Other salesmen of poor-value policies will be obliged to study their competition or change their occupation. The public can only benefit.

Perhaps one of the most profound advertisements for the industry was carried by the graffiti wall at a British university. It read: 'Life Assurance takes over where you leave off'.

Lloyd's of London

An underwriter is an insurance specialist who
accepts a premium to provide protection
against capital punishment.

Anon.

Still recovering from the Great Fire, London was slowly
becoming accustomed to its first street lamps; war was
raging between France and Spain, and mindless massacres
were again the vogue in Turkey. Both the Bank of England
and the Hudson Bay Company had recently received their
charters, and slavery was still a flourishing business in the
British Colonies.

On the personal front, John Churchill, the Duke of Marl-
borough, had been banished from England, wrongly
accused of treason, the Duke of York was busy preaching
Catholicism, while John Bunyan sat in jail polishing up a
synopsis for *The Pilgrim's Progress.* Rembrandt had recently
died after being declared a bankrupt, and Thomas Coutts
was shortly to open his own banking house. The zero rate of
inflation was to remain unchanged for another hundred
years.

It was against this background that Lloyd's Coffee House
made its appearance in London's Tower Street in 1688, the
year that the bloodless revolution brought William and Mary
to the throne of England. Unfortunately, history tells us little
either about Edward Lloyd or his famous coffee house. It
was one of many such establishments and, apart from odd
references in contemporary City news-sheets, the record is
blank. The first mention of Lloyd's appears in a London
gazette of the late 1690s, in which an advertisement
appeared offering a guinea reward for information regarding
stolen watches. The address given was that of Edward
Lloyd's Coffee House in Tower Street.

It seems very likely that in those days before newspapers,
Edward Lloyd provided trustworthy shipping news to the

merchants, ships' captains and shipowners who patronized his coffee shop. This useful intelligence was one of the basic ingredients for successful underwriting and ensured that Lloyd's Coffee House became the recognized place for obtaining marine insurance cover.

Edward Lloyd died in 1713, having left his name, and the coffee house that bore it, to posterity. He had contented himself with providing congenial surroundings for his patrons, and is not known ever himself to have taken part in underwriting. The Corporation of Lloyd's, as it is known today, was actually created by an Act of Parliament in 1871, by which time it had established its name and had forged a remarkable reputation for its own integrity and that of its members. It was no small achievement to have survived both the American War of Independence and some twenty years of fighting with France with a name synonymous with reliability.

Three centuries ago, brokers hawked their risks around the City of London inviting those with sufficient means to take a share in return for a percentage of the premium. As it was then, so it is today. Every single Lloyd's policy is underwritten by private individuals with unlimited liability: no corporation, regardless of its size or financial reserves, can be a Member or participate in its profits or business activities. The method of underwriting is the same only in principle, however — the enterprising merchant of the past, signing policies in a coffee house as a sideline to his main business, has long ago given way to the professional underwriter employed by others to accept business at Lloyd's on their behalf. Today, with nearly thirty thousand of them, the Members of Lloyd's are grouped into some five hundred syndicates, varying in size from just a few to more than fifteen hundred Members (known as Names) each one of them a member of up to as many as forty syndicates. Nowhere in the world is there so much collective underwriting expertise under one roof as at Lloyd's. Good faith undoubtedly characterizes the special relationship between broker and underwriter each of whom recognizes the necessity to place complete trust in the other. Without such mutual trust, Lloyd's would not long survive and would

certainly not be handling a premium income of more than
£10,000,000 every working day of the year. Its pride and
success lie in its reputation to settle claims, not just more
fairly than most insurers, but more speedily. The earthquake
that hit San Francisco in 1906 brought ruin to many US
insurers and practically destroyed the world insurance
market. Members of Lloyd's paid out a cool $100,000,000
and indelibly established its name for integrity and reliability.
The American market today provides over 60 per cent of all
Lloyd's business and continues to look to Lloyd's to lead
many of its largest risks, among them the Space Shuttle, with
all its inherent dangers and liabilities. When all seven astro-
nauts on the *Challenger* were killed in the tragic accident
early in 1986, Lloyd's paid out the accident compensation in
twenty-four hours — the compensation on the life of the one
woman aboard the spacecraft alone amounted to
£1,000,000. It is in pioneering and large-risk projects, such
as space missions or nuclear bases, that this three-hundred-
year-old establishment leads the world insurance market. Its
actual percentage of world business has, however, fallen —
yet, strangely enough, its premium income has grown more
than tenfold in recent years; and in spite of the fact that it
may underwrite less than ten per cent of the world's marine
business, its role as world leader in that area has remained
unchanged and virtually unchallenged.

But all has not been well at Lloyd's in recent times. To
echoes of disbelief, shame hit this insurance Mecca in the
early 1980s. It had nothing to do with claims, arson, air
crashes or hurricanes — the shock that vibrated throughout
the world's greatest insurance centre was created by
unthinkable and shattering evidence of embezzlement, fraud
and financial intrigue. A previously respected syndicate, No.
900, had been grossly mismanaged. Furthermore, the
underwriter and Agent, a certain Peter Cameron Webb, and
his deputy had quietly and cleverly misappropriated some
£40,000,000 before disappearing overseas. If ever there was
reason to ring the Lutine Bell this must have been it. But that
famous souvenir from the HMS *Lutine*, wrecked in 1799,
remained silent. Erected in the centre of the Underwriting
Room to obtain hush for announcements of special interest,

no one was prepared to ring it for in-house piracy. But this was not a story to be hushed up or disguised for the Press. Fifteen hundred Names, including the Chairman of Lloyd's and a member of the Royal family were among the losers. It was tranquillizer time for Members of the Committee of Lloyd's, who suddenly realized how badly they needed PR consultants. The news was pure champagne for the media, which gave it more mileage than had ever been given to the Pope or any sex stories emanating from the Palace. But worse was to come.

Apart from the swindle, the actual underwriting performance itself made many question the sanity of the underwriter. Irresponsible and reckless acceptance of large shares of hazardous risks produced some of the worst individual losses known to Lloyd's. By the time the aggregate figures reached £100,000,000 many Members were too paralysed with shock to realize that they were ruined. Blame hit the fan from all angles, with newspaper hacks and TV commentators exhaling wind, recriminations and impressive sounding drivel. Those who viewed hindsight as a qualification were able to indicate precisely how the ghastly business might have been avoided. The battle of wits and rights will no doubt be fought for long enough to make fortunes for the lawyers but, at the end of the day, the Names can only be losers. That is, apart from Mr Cameron Webb who is still basking in luxury in the sun.

To keep the record straight, the circumstances that led to the fiasco were bizarre. They date back to the years when underwriting profits, mostly classified as unearned income, were taxed at 98 per cent. In practice, this means that every £1,000 placed in reserves, for future claims, was costing Members of Lloyd's only £20. It made good sense, therefore, to stack up reserves in every way possible against the time when heavy claims might appear. It did not require too much ingenuity to establish a re-insurance network to accept vast premiums for rainy days. The system simply required a no-risk company to be set up to accept premiums as though they were taking part of the risk. As anticipated, neither the syndicate accountants nor Lloyd's itself bothered to check the bona fides of the bogus re-insurance companies owned by Mr Cameron Webb and his partner. The odd quirk was that the rainy days never arrived and the tax-free reserves grew like Topsy. Eventually, Cameron Webb reckoned that he had amassed sufficient millions and was overdue for retirement. Without a word to anyone except his accomplice, he packed his bags and flew to Gibraltar and thence to Bermuda, where he calmly removed millions of pounds and dollars from the accounts of the re-insurance companies. For sheer gall, it was an impressive performance.

Suddenly, the most exclusive and respected club in the world, which had never reneged on a claim throughout its three-hundred-year-old history, whose expertise and skill were second only to its integrity, became the target of every left-wing politician, pseudo-economist and financial guru seeking self-exposure. But criticism was justified. Because nothing like it had ever happened before, the hierarchy of Lloyd's had been certain that it could never happen. It simply never occurred to anyone that a business whose turnover had grown from £100,000,000 to over £3,000,000,000 in only twenty years might be in need of self-examination and greater monitoring. Wise, experienced, shrewd, cautious, calculating underwriters at Lloyd's, accustomed to investigating every type of hazard and risk in the world, had never contemplated the possibility of fraud perpetrated by actual members of the Club.

In perspective, how could it be foreseen? There are no excuses masquerading as reasons. Things like that did not happen in Lime Street, but now no amount of plastic accountancy will remove the scars. Looking back, some may find it surprising that it did not happen earlier. Others may be amazed that an umbrella organization, with nearly five hundred autonomous associated member-groups, handling a £3,000,000,000 turnover, should be so severely shaken by a handful of rogues. On investigation it was discovered that, coincidentally, one or two smaller fry were playing the same game as Cameron Webb. What is interesting is the shock and the sheer numbness suffered by those closely connected with the Lloyd's market. Any other worldwide organization that suffered dishonesty losses of 1 per cent of turnover would hardly rate three lines on the back pages of the financial Press. The big difference is that nobody ever expected it of Lloyd's. Despite the furore, the horrific disclosures have not discouraged more people than ever from applying for Membership, and new business continues to flow into the market.

Those with unblemished characters and liquid assets of £100,000 are usually eligible to become underwriting Members — Names — of Lloyd's. Contrary to popular belief, however, one cannot simply walk into this establishment and declare one's interest in joining the brotherhood of risk-takers. Every Member, without exception, has to be represented by an underwriting Agent who, in turn, is approved by the Committee of Lloyd's. These Agents — all men known to be knowledgeable, experienced, and familiar with the workings of Lloyd's — do not advertise; rather, they acquire their clients through recommendations from Lloyd's brokers, chartered accountants, bank managers, or other Members of Lloyd's. Failing such contacts, the Registrar at Lloyd's will generally be prepared to provide a shortlist of Agents who are pleased to be helpful. Although the Agents operate quite independently, they are obliged to follow principles laid down by the Committee of Lloyd's, and have to submit their accounts to Lloyd's for approval every year.

The Agent's main function is to act in the best interests of each Name by producing a well-balanced portfolio of syndicates; it is also in his own interest, as most of his income is derived from a share in the underwriting profit and investment income enjoyed by his clients. In addition, he receives a small share of the annual fee (1 per cent of the total premiums underwritten for him) which every Name has to pay the underwriter who accepts him or her in his syndicate.

Each Member is virtually a one-man (or woman) insurance company with *unlimited* liability, which means that he or she is in the risk business up to his or her last penny. It is the responsibility of the Agent to make this clear orally and in writing. Eventually, when, just before being admitted, the Name attends an obligatory meeting with the Chairman of Lloyd's or his representative on the Committee, it is again emphasized that he or she who joins Lloyd's places his or her entire fortune on the nail. It is for this reason that many effect Stop Loss Policies, which are designed to take the sting out of any catastrophic claim beyond £20,000. Even these contracts usually carry a limit of £100,000 but this proved more than adequate until certain underwriters went berserk in the 1980s, accepting risks at ridiculously low premiums which they subsequently re-insured with the off-shore companies set up by Cameron Webb and his partner.

The rules are identical for each Member who, individually, takes his share of the profits and the losses of every syndicate he joins. The minimum deposit required by every Name is £25,000 which can be provided by way of quoted securities or bank guarantees. This entitles a Name to have premiums accepted on his behalf, by one or more underwriters, up to £100,000. The figures are pro-rata up to a maximum premium income of £1,000,000.

A wise Name will endeavour to be a member of as many syndicates as his premium income will sensibly allow. Only an ill-advised gambler would place more than a small percentage of his total commitment in the hands of a single underwriter, however good the man's reputation or profit record. A new Member should make it his business to study syndicate figures and meet all the underwriters acting for him; and he must remember that Lloyd's makes money when its premiums received for underwriting dangerous perils exceed the claims — but that it need not always be this way. The more syndicates included in an underwriting portfolio, therefore, the greater the chances of steady profits.

On balance, most underwriting Members have good reason to be grateful to their Agents and their underwriters. In normal times, a Name enjoys all the income on his deposited investments, a reasonable underwriting profit, plus the investment income which arises from premiums that are invested pending their distribution to settle claims or pay out profits. It is not surprising that wealthy Americans have been queuing to join Lloyd's ever since foreigners were first admitted as Members in 1969.

Those who fear nightmares about air crashes, plagues and oil fires should stay away from underwriting. These are the very risks for which underwriters accept premiums every day in the hope that all calamities won't arrive at the same time.

The worst claim that many at Lloyd's can imagine would involve two packed Jumbo jets, each carrying a multimillion cargo, colliding and crashing down onto New York. Such a catastrophe, in isolation, is likely to cost the average Name no more than a few hundred pounds. This relatively small loss reflects the strength and wisdom of re-insurance — laying off some of the risk, in book-making terms, but although the principle is the same, re-insurance in the insurance world is a very sophisticated business, and competent re-insurance brokers are highly qualified technicians whose expertise puts them among the highest paid at Lloyd's and in the international insurance market generally.

The one-off catastrophe, like an airline disaster or a hurricane, is normally built into the premium calculations of any underwriter. If, however, there were too many such calamities in any one year, there would be a shortage of shirts in Lloyd's. Most large losses are suffered as a result of overoptimistic underwriters who forget to consider the worst rather than the most likely. One example of sheer stupidity was the policy written to protect computer-leasing whereby compensation was paid if lessees broke their contracts. There is no such thing as the right premium in instances like this where it is impossible to assess the risk, and many underwriters who subscribed to the cover lost a fortune for the Names.

Such is underwriting in Lime Street. It generates over £3,000,000,000 a year in foreign currency, and as an industry is by far the largest buyer and holder of government securities in the country. No sane political party would interfere with it just so long as it regulates itself to maintain the highest standards in commercial practice.

A MIXED HA'PORTH

Lateral Thinking

Think before you think.

J. Stanislaw

Lateral thinking — the phrase and the idea behind it brought to the public consciousness by Edward de Bono, the eminent psychologist — can, in its simplest form, be described as a method of developing logical answers to a wide variety of problems. As opposed to vertical thinking, which is traditional, disciplined and predictable, lateral thinking is original, creative and exploratory. The two are complementary, but it is the vertical thinker who develops the ideas generated by the lateral thinker.

In the political field there is constant evidence of planning by those schooled to think along prescribed lines — highly experienced and competent men, many of whose able brains were trained to stretch only within the confines of mental strait-jackets. When a group of Americans was held hostage by the Iranian religious fanatic, Ayatollah Khomeini, the President of the United States and his advisers were at their wits' end. The CIA had never considered the possibility of such an event, and consequently were completely un-prepared; with all the economic power of the greatest coun-try in the Western hemisphere, there was no one around with any worthwhile muscle to negotiate on their behalf. The hostages remained imprisoned while secret meetings took place between the powers that control the Senate, the

Treasury and the American army and its intelligence network.

No outside opinions were sought. The obvious answer, to the Americans, was a rescue operation and, inspired by the success of the Entebbe exercise, plans began to take shape. Decisions were made regarding the means of attack; the numbers of rescuers involved; the type of aircraft, armoured vehicles and ammunition to be used, and, above all, the timing. Eventually, the blueprint was ready and the count-down began for the highly trained team to descend on Iran and rescue the twenty-odd hostages. A determination to succeed was all the Americans had in common with the Israeli team who had created history in Uganda. The operation was doomed before it began and, in the event, proved to be a ghastly and humiliating failure.

Later, an American diplomat asked the Israeli Chief of Staff where he thought the operation had gone wrong. The latter slowly went over the exercise as he saw it. The location was extremely difficult. It was a long way from an airport for fifty rescuers and twenty hostages who were quite unfamiliar with the country. Even though the Americans are superior soldiers, the prison was far better guarded than they had been led to believe. No allowance had been made for error or casualties. The thinking was all wrong.

'And what would you have done?' enquired the diplomat.

'We would have kidnapped the Ayatollah,' replied the Chief of Staff.

The multimillion-dollar investment in the rescue exercise was completely irrelevant. The yards of reportage that covered every newspaper in the world mentioned every single political and emotional aspect but, just for once, there was no reference to money. Fortunately that had not come into either vertical or lateral thinking.

But the world of money and business must surely offer the greatest number of opportunities for the successful application of the principle identified and developed by de Bono. The following examples are, perhaps, more obvious than most but they have been intentionally chosen to illustrate how the presentation of facts can dictate thinking processes.

EXAMPLE 1

A printing company spends £500,000 on a new machine which has a capacity to produce long runs of small documents at four times the speed of other machines. Five years later, the company is encouraged to buy, for £1,000,000, a vastly superior machine, which, in addition to maintaining the speed, will also print larger documents in several colours. As an encouragement to make the purchase, the company is offered £50,000 in part exchange for its old machine. While considering the proposition, the company receives another offer to rent out the old machine at £20,000 a year for five years. Ideally, the company would prefer to keep the old machine as a back-up but, as this would involve spending a further £200,000 to house the new machine, this idea is dismissed. Bearing in mind that the company can readily fund the £1,000,000 expenditure which will substantially increase its profits, which of the offers should it accept? For the purpose of the exercise, tax considerations should be ignored.

The first offer of an immediate sum of £50,000 has the distinct advantage of tidiness. Acceptance would immediately close the deal and leave no open ends. On the other hand, assuming that the covenant of the lessee is sound, it would appear to make good sense to accept the second offer. This would provide an excellent return, and the cost of collecting the rent would be nominal.

In the event, the company ignored both offers and destroyed the machine. Either of the other alternatives would have given a competitor the opportunity to create competition for a relatively modest investment.

EXAMPLE 2

A middle-aged couple plan an extensive holiday to the Far East at a cost of £5,000. Their agent recommends a holiday insurance which, for £50, will provide compensation of £100,000 each if their lives are lost in a plane accident. Looking into the matter more carefully, the man discovers that, as an American Express Card-holder, he could obtain the same accident cover for £40. His problem is whether to bother to make special arrangements for the sake of saving

£10. Furthermore, he is conscious of the enormous amount of trouble taken by the agent and does not want to appear cheese-paring. His other thoughts are:

1   Should he ignore the additional cost as a small price to pay for tidiness?
2   Should he increase the cheaper premium to have the benefit of higher protection?

What the man should really be asking himself is why do he and his wife need that amount of accident insurance. Cheap or dear, does he really want to leave anyone an additional £200,000, bearing in mind that the airline provides an automatic insurance of £75,000 for each passenger? In addition, practically every heir in history has sought compensation from the aircraft manufacturer that built a passenger plane that crashed. There is nothing like incineration in an aircraft to make even the most distant relation become emotional about compensation. Figures show that, on average, such claimants can reckon on another £100,000 for their own distress. On this basis, the couple planning their holiday will leave their beneficiaries around £350,000 in the event of an air crash. They don't need to go bargain-hunting for aviation-accident insurance.

EXAMPLE 3
The chairman of an engineering company is under pressure to diversify into marketing computers for shop-keepers. The theories are:

1   There are several hundred thousand shop-keepers.
2   The market is practically untapped.
3   The price of each computer is so low as to obviate any need to give credit.

The two most favoured products, which are priced the same, are manufactured abroad. The one from Sweden has the advantage of coming to agents with three months' credit. The one from Germany has two advantages: it is quite well known, having sold several thousand already in this country; and a London-based company has the agency for spares — thus goodwill can be enhanced by delays being avoided in the event of breakdowns. The board is divided, one half valuing the credit line, the other half conscious of the value of service. The decision is left to the chairman.

He decided on the German product, provided that he was successful in a separate negotiation to buy the company with the spare-parts agency.

Broadly speaking, entrepreneurs, business self-starters and salesmen are likely to be lateral thinkers. Administrators, civil servants, company secretaries and army officers are likely to be vertical thinkers. The two groups complement each other, for those in the former category invariably need those in the latter to develop and implement their ideas.

House Purchase

Owning a house with your wife gives you
something to share when you break up.
Will Rodgers

Throughout the last fifty years, leaving aside the aberrant period of the Second World War, the vast majority of those owning their own homes have found it their greatest long-term investment. Except in certain distressed areas, houses have more than kept pace with inflation and often provided their owners with an asset out of all proportion to their standard of living. That is to say that there are many who could not contemplate buying their present house at today's market price. While prices in the north of England have always been lower than those in the south, their rate of appreciation has only varied in the more affluent areas. A house in the north which cost £5,000 in 1965 might well have been worth £75,000 in 1985. The same house in London, having cost £10,000 twenty years ago, would probably be valued at nearer £200,000. This unprecedented appreciation has enabled many to enjoy more comfortable retirement by switching to smaller and cheaper homes or by moving to less expensive areas. Subsequently, unimaginable sums have been inherited. On the other hand, for those who, for one reason or another, have to move into a larger home, it can cause hardship or force them to move farther from the city centre.

Against this background is a greater number of young, first-time house buyers in England than anywhere else in Europe. Renting a property is no longer seen as a practical arrangement and, conversely, the cost of building and refurbishing accommodation for renting has made it an unattractive proposition for property developers. As a result, the mortgage market has boomed, encouraging both insurance companies and banks to compete with building societies for new business. In the broadest possible terms, mortgages are normally provided over periods of fifteen to thirty years with repayment being made by regular monthly instalments or through the medium of an endowment policy. Now that life-assurance premiums no longer enjoy preferential tax treatment many must find it more economical to arrange straightforward repayment mortgages. A reducing term assurance policy which will always repay the outstanding mortgage, in the event of death, is a very cheap and effective way of providing adequate protection. This contract should be compared with a fire policy which provides essential cover, so long as premiums are paid, but offers no return of premium if there is no claim. For the better-off, a with-bonus endowment policy can be a very profitable way of repaying the loan. The difference on a £20,000 loan is likely to be in the region of £2-300 a year, and this could well produce a profit of at least £20,000 at the end of twenty years.

The burden of a mortgage on a young couple in the early years of their marriage frequently demands many sacrifices and can impose unanticipated pressures on their relationship. Most young first-time buyers find that they are financially over-stretched initially but, with promotion and salary increments, are able to cope fairly comfortably after the first few years. It is this difficult period which often justifies a mortgage being arranged with a bank. While building societies and insurance companies offer a variety of mortgage facilities, the banks are traditionally more flexible. All things being equal — namely the value of the property, and the covenant of the purchaser being satisfactory — it is often easier to prevail on a bank to tailor-make a mortgage package. This is particularly so as they are less known in the field, and are eager to build a reputation for helping property owners — a class of person among the most responsible and likeliest to be a reliable long-term bank customer. A further advantage of a bank mortgage is that it is possible to reduce the outstanding amount, with less hassle, if a windfall ever arrives.

Perhaps the most beneficial mortgage arrangement for those with limited capital is one which allows interest only for the first five years. During this period there are no capital repayments whatsoever and the outgoings on a £30,000 mortgage could be reduced by as much as £120 a month compared with an average building society arrangement. Of course, it does mean that interest will be paid for more years, but the net cost in the early years would be substantially lower, especially as the interest can be offset against tax; by the time capital repayments fall due, it is reasonably likely that the house-owner will be better able to afford them.

The secret of finding the most suitable mortgage arrangement is to shop around and never to assume that all those in the business offer similar terms. For most people it is likely to be the largest single financial arrangement which they will ever make and it justifies careful thought and research. And it is worth bearing in mind that many people move from their first house within four years, not necessarily because they need somewhere bigger but because they suddenly realize the importance of living closer to shops, friends, relations, transport, schools, or their jobs.

Building Societies

The house was more covered with mortgages
than with paint.

George Ade

The philosophy of home ownership owes more to the building society movement than any other financial institution. Dating back to the early nineteenth century, building societies were established to provide long-term mortgages for house-purchase and offer attractive returns for small savers. The secret of the exercise has been the special tax treatment which successive governments have granted these societies. For more than a hundred years, neither banks nor insurance companies wanted to compete for this class of business. Anyone requiring a mortgage automatically sought one from a building society knowing that they could borrow for a fixed term of years without fear of the loan being suddenly recalled.

Today, the principle remains the same but, with rising wages and soaring house prices, the competition for mortgage business has moved from neutral into a high gear. Banks, desperate for new business and a better image, have trespassed on this territory in an effort to increase the numbers of their customers. The great advantage of a bank mortgage is its flexibility and the opportunity to raise further loans as the value of the house increases. This facility is not usually available from other mortgagors. Insurance companies too have muscled into this lucrative market to create further opportunities to sell both endowment and fire policies. Unlike building societies, that normally require repayments through equal monthly instalments of capital and interest, insurance companies charge interest only, with the actual repayment being made through an endowment policy for the full term of the mortgage. For many, this is by far the most attractive method as, in addition to life insurance, it affords the individual the opportunity to enjoy

the bonuses on a policy in fact effected to repay a mortgage. A policy to repay a mortgage of £20,000, for example, repaid through a with-bonus endowment plan, might
well cost an extra £200 a year for twenty years, but
could ultimately produce a net tax-free profit of around
£20,000.

Unfortunately, tax relief on interest is only allowed on a
mortgage up to £30,000. Above this figure, the cost of a
mortgage becomes prohibitive and throws an enormous
financial strain, particularly on first-time purchasers. Unless
the government raises this figure, more and more young
marrieds are likely to be obliged to live many miles from
their places of employment, which involves high travelling
costs and considerable time wastage. Yet, while hundreds of
thousands of commuters have no choice in the matter, there
are just as many who are happy to accept the strain in order
to work in big cities rather than nearer to home. What is
more surprising is that with all its financial muscle the Building Society Association appears to be doing so little to lobby
the government to raise the limits for tax relief. In many
areas property values have more than doubled since the tax
relief limit of £30,000 was first agreed.

The investment side of the business of building societies
offers first-class opportunities for those wishing to save or
invest with security. Although tax on the interest earned is
deducted at source and can never be recovered, the comparative net returns, coupled with their excellent record, make
building societies attractive for most investors. Those who
are paying less than the basic (30 per cent) rate of tax,
however, might well examine other opportunities for investment: a combination of Savings Certificates, Post Office
Saving and National Savings Deposit Bonds could well
produce a much higher overall return. Ideally, money
invested in Savings Certificates should be left there for five
years if possible, particularly as the capital growth is guaranteed; the first £70 earned from Post Office Savings Accounts
is completely tax-free and makes it a worthwhile investment for
ready money; National Saving Bonds provide a higher-than-
average return for money which one does not expect to need
for at least one year, and, furthermore, the interest is payable

gross without any deductions at all.

All building societies which are members of the Building Society Association virtually carry a guarantee that your savings are safe with them. But terms do vary, competition is keen and it can be worthwhile to compare rates before deciding where to deposit your hard-earned savings. If in any doubt, Abbey National, with over a hundred branches in London alone, and offices throughout the country, will always give good value for money. For very many, this society, with its outstanding reputation, its vast resources and its impressive organization, more than compensates for the odd extra per cent which might be available elsewhere from time to time.

Neither the British government, the banks nor the most conservative investors feel that members of the Building Society Association should carry insurance protection against loss of deposits as do savings institutions and mortgage funds in America. On the very rare occasions when a small building society has failed, other societies have immediately guaranteed the deposits of any customers left stranded. To ensure the security of your money in any building society, that society's membership of the Building Society association is an essential prerequisite.

First-time house-buyers who have been saving for a deposit for their first home can often secure a guaranteed mortgage advance from the society with which they have been saving regularly – a very important consideration in a market that has often experienced a shortage of mortgage funds. The time must surely come when, in an effort to assist first-time home-buyers, building societies and others in this market will – supported by guarantees of the buyers' bona fides from well-established employers – grant 100 per cent mortgages against suitable properties. This would not only ease the strain for many young, responsible people and increase the loyalty of those enjoying the privilege, but it would also be very good business. Indeed, in these days of competitive package deals, it could make a great deal of sense for a large building society to join forces with a major life office. Together, they could grant 100 per cent mortgages, and arrange special discounts and hire-purchase terms with reputable house furnishers for their customers. This could be another coup for Great Universal Stores, the group which certainly understands mass-marketing and the benefits of discount trading.

Credit Cards

It is not in my interest to pay the principal;
nor is it my principle to pay the interest.
Richard Brinsley Sheridan

It is understandable that millions of people find credit cards
a great financial convenience. Apart from relieving the
necessity of carrying cash, they enable many to succumb to
impulse-buying, and thus acquire goods which they can ill
afford or well do without. This is the real bait which encourages retailers to pay a commission — usually 5 per cent — to
banks and other card operators. As well as making it that
much easier for buyers to yield to temptation, there is
another advantage to retailers — credit-card operators are
not known to bounce cheques. Many retailers see the commission they have to pay as insurance for guaranteed payment — a major improvement on the days when practically
every customer's cheque presented a possible commercial
risk. Thus a medium-sized restaurant might serve to card-
paying customers an average of two hundred meals a day
five days a week; even at only £10 a meal, this produces a
guaranteed turnover of about £500,000 a year, and a possible return to the credit-card bank of as much as £25,000.

This, however, is only half the happy story of why banks
compete for the business. The other half is the special rate
of interest they charge their clients whose accounts are not
paid in full and promptly: Shylock would be absolved from
any accusations of usury. In reality, rates have been over 20
per cent at times when standard borrowing terms were less
than half that, and as they are not normally allowable for tax
relief, the pre-tax rate can be equivalent to 50 per cent when
compared with bank loans. In his halcyon days Edward
Heath might well have described this as the unacceptable
face of capitalism, but in the world of the moneylenders it is
acceptable.

The obvious assumption is that taxpayers know better

than to accept these terms, but statistics do not bear this out
— indeed, they point to the contrary. None the less there are
two simple ways of enjoying the use of credit cards and
exploiting the system.

The first is sufficiently obvious to have been overlooked
by the majority and most bank managers do not believe it is
within their province to mention it to their customers. The
simple fact is that it is far cheaper to open an overdraft
account than to pay credit-card interest rates. Broadly speaking, an annual turnover of £2,000, with an average debit
balance of £300 can easily save a net £30 a year. It is worth
remembering that this is equivalent to £70 in top tax-rate
terms and most people still go a long way to save this sort of
money. But perhaps the customer is about to get a better
deal — frantic competition is with us, and it may just occur
to one of the more desperate contenders that fair trading is
good business. The Big Bang is allegedly designed to free
the finance world of its shackles, illusory though they may
be — what a fabulous opportunity for a building society to
offer 'plastic services' at really competitive rates — the day
might even come when such an institution, far from charging interest, will agree to share the retailers' discount with
the credit-card customers. Come the millenium.

In the meantime, it may be profitable to borrow from
building societies in order to repay bank loans or, sometimes, vice-versa; whoever the lender, he is likely to be more
sympathetic to granting a loan to pay for a holiday, double-
glazing, or even car maintenance, than to pay off credit-card
usurers.

The second method of getting the best out of the credit-
card system requires more nerve but the practice will grow
quickly as confidence increases with success. Simply pay by
cash but exhibit your credit card to obtain the same discount as the bank. Such a method of payment should be
readily acceptable when you point out that it does after all
give the retailer or restaurateur the immediate settlement
which he does not usually get from the bank. A 5 per cent
discount on a £100 restaurant bill for example, can be equal
to £12 in gross income terms; those who question its value
should measure it against the *extra* tip they are prepared to

give. The practice is prevalent on the Continent, and it can pay off equally well in this country. The moral of the exercise is simply to remember that there are no prizes for the timid.

It is always important not to have any conscience about banks and other professional moneylenders. They understand the money game so much better than you do. It is as well to bear in mind what every little fish knows — there is no such creature as a friendly shark.

The Carpet Story

Be extravagant — it's cheaper.
Chinese proverb.

The only sad thing about bargains is that they are usually so expensive. When a solvent business man starts selling £100 articles for £50, don't try and work it out. It's invariably more profitable to reckon that he's one step ahead of you, and to keep walking. The secret of his success is that most people don't.

Prices of even the finest-quality fitted carpets, for instance, vary considerably. One store will give away the underfelt simply to increase its turnover; another will make less profit in order to make room for new designs, and then, of course, there is the regular closing-down sale.

Mostly, people sell carpets to make money, and there are not so many insurance claims in the carpet business to justify the size of some of the reductions offered to the public. If the quality is good and the company is sound, then question their apparent benevolence. (This, of course, applies to other goods, too.) By all means let one of the 'top-quality-cheap-price' firms quote for your fitted carpets. Then take the order to one of the big stores who are offering exactly the same carpet, of the same quality, at a higher price. Let them quote too. Often they offer the better bargain because they employ people who measure more accurately: from the first retailer, you might end up buying 100 yards at £12 per yard, which will cost you £1,200; but from the second you might buy just 80 yards at £13 per yard, which comes to £1,040 — thus, by going to the 'more expensive' firm, you save £160.

Of course there are many honest traders, but it costs nothing to check. If estimates are not free, keep walking.

Exactly the same principle should be applied with curtains, upholstery, major mail-order items and first and second mortgage arrangements. The real bargains in the goods section are obtained by settling for top quality with a first-class house and then negotiating the highest discount. Far from being unreasonable, you will simply be following the practice which the best retailers adopt with manufacturers. Cheap money offers such as loans at apparently low interest rates, should always be checked with your bank and, if necessary, a second bank.

Selling Charity

Remember the poor — it costs nothing.
Josh Billings' (Henry Wheeler Shaw)

Any definition of poverty must depend on the location of
the observer and his ability to focus his telescope. It is quite
erroneous to believe that many of the better-offs turn a blind
eye to the poverty-stricken and the hungry. They don't.
That's the eye they keep on their self-indulgences. In his
magnum opus, Inquiries concerning The Poor, the Reverend John McFarlane endeavoured to prove 'that the greatest
number of those who are objects of charity are such as have
reduced themselves to this situation by sloth and vice'.
Revelling in his enlightened philosophy, he continued: '... in
most cases, a modest degree of frugality might have prevented indigence.' Inebriated with his own convictions, this
learned eighteenth-century cleric then inspired a scholarly
game for the amusement and edification of his humble
colleagues. In considering the needs of desperate paupers,
he and his friends had to guess which were blameworthy
and which were blameless. 'It is imperative that we learn to
recognize shiftlessness and insobriety,' wrote the reverend
gentleman in his book of rules.

But, fortunately, there are many people in England who
believe that abject poverty is unacceptable in a world of
comparative affluence. Sympathetic though these people
may be, however, animals in distress take pride of place in
their hearts and pockets. Converting benevolence into cash
in 1984, charitable members of the British public gave seven
times as much to animal aid societies as they did to those
concerned with the sick, the handicapped, the old and those
suffering in famine-infested countries. Sadly, the vast majority base their attitudes on assumptions, and their conclusions on misconceptions. Few realize that, apart from the
deprived and the impoverished, somewhere in the world
four hundred God-created people die of hunger every hour,

twenty-four hours a day. These are not even among the registered poor — they are the forsaken who are dying from birth. According to the 1984 Report of the World Bank, there are over 500,000,000 human beings living in dire poverty somewhere on this good earth. There are reckoned to be a further 300,000,000 who, grossly undernourished and medically neglected, are likely to die young. Even in the United States, where money is synonymous with culture, there are many who starve in shacks and slums. Quoting from the *Baltimore Sun*, in March 1985, The *New York Herald Tribune* makes reference to twenty million Americans who are desperately hungry for long periods of each month. This shattering fact was disclosed in the same week that the President formally approved a fresh nuclear budget of $1,500,000,000.

In terms of human misery and degradation, the starving millions and the battalions of the forgotten poor serve to illustrate the comparative indifference of the majority, and the moral insensibilities of the rich. To consider poverty in perspective, it might be helpful to record definitions given by learned clergy at an Ecumenical Conference in London in 1981: there were those who felt that the man without three meals a day was poor; others maintained a man should have adequate shelter and food before he can graduate to a different category; and some felt that food, shelter and clothing were equally essential. A purist suggested that any man without a margin to help his neighbour must be considered poor. 'We must aim,' concluded a bishop, 'to abolish starvation in the world and stabilize misery.' No one was sure whether he considered stabilization started or stopped at those who famish in squalor for lack of 80p a week.

When in 436BC in Rome, famine drove thousands of desperate souls to throw themselves into the Tiber, only the gladiators declared a day of mourning. Such are the stories studied by historians and economists before they conclude that hopelessness must perpetually dog the footsteps of the suffering masses. The expenditure of vast research grants has barely changed the pessimistic view of the statisticians, that only the Almighty Himself can alleviate human tragedy on a grand scale.

In the meantime, irrigation experts continue their fight to make the world's deserts green, inhibited by political intrigue and the vested interests of the more affluent members of the farming fraternity. In the EEC, the authorities convert millions of tonnes of cereals into plastics on the pretext of having insufficient warehouse room. Desperately afraid of falling prices, European farmers burn mountains of grain, and helpless theologians continue to invest in prayer. Allegedly, the cost of shipping grain to starving Africa is too high for the affluent to contemplate.

Fortunately, there is also a happier side to the charity picture. There are dozens of worthy charities like War on Want, the NSPCC, Oxfam, and many others, dedicated to relieve poverty and suffering at home and throughout the distressed areas of the world. There are others, like The Royal Commonwealth Society for the Blind, who specialize in bringing medical treatment to parts of the Third World where hundreds of thousands suffer with blindness. A donation of a mere £100 is enough to restore the gift of sight to more than 100 human beings. There are organizations, such as Winged Fellowship, who provide holidays for the chair- and the bed-ridden; The Malcolm Sargent Cancer Fund For Children, which offers a magnificent welfare service from which 5,000 children benefit every year, and there are numerous others. But they only touch the peripheries of the needy. The problem is always the same: insufficient funds. All is not lost, however; so long as there are enough people who care, a great deal more can be achieved. If any proof of what one individual can achieve is necessary, it was certainly provided in 1985 by the pop singer, Bob Geldof. While governments were making grants of a few millions to help the suffering in Ethiopia, Bob decided that the man in the street could be roused to recognize a moral obligation to relieve the unprecedented suffering in that forsaken country. He did just that by promoting a single concert which raised over £40,000,000 for that one cause: exactly four times as much as the United States Senate authorized for the same area of distress. Bob is certainly a one-off in England, but there are others who have made and continue to make remarkable contributions to alleviate suffering. Perhaps the most unlikely is Ryoichi Sasakawa, an ex-Fascist and Japanese war criminal, who, having amassed one of the largest fortunes in the world, claimed to have given away $12,000,000,000 to charity, albeit through businesses built on government orders.

In the context of this chapter the question must be asked, could charity be sold more effectively to those able to give it? The answer must surely be in the affirmative.

Initially, a small comparison may assist in helping one to see the position in focus. In England, a compassionate local authority, making a holiday grant to a poor child, will rightly include £15 a week for Coca-Cola and fun. What many cannot comprehend is that the same amount provides a survival kit for a starving person for nearly twenty weeks.

Now, the top thirty British companies, comprising the *Financial Times* Index, make an aggregate pre-tax profit of £11,273,000,000. In the United States, those corporations comprising the Dow Jones Index make $54,000,000,000. A voluntary tax of only 1 per cent would produce £650,000,000 without affecting the lifestyle of a single shareholder or employee. If the practice were generally adopted throughout the Western hemisphere, the overall benefit could exceed £4,000,000,000 per annum. This kind of money could build quite a few miles of water pipes and rescue many millions of tons of grain from the food pyres of Europe. Even the wealthy farmers, desperate to preserve their profit margins, would not suffer. Furthermore, it could be fabulous publicity for companies to use their advertisements to mention how much they spend helping the deprived and the despondent.

On a personal level, the average secretary takes home around £400 a month. Just 1 per cent of this could actually keep a human being alive. The potential for the development of this theme is endless. Is it conceivable that the majority would refuse? Could the Post Office be prevailed upon to sell Charity Stamps to help countless thousands of generous people, not wealthy enough to make substantial contributions, nevertheless to give to the causes of their choice? Their contributions in aggregate could easily meet or overtake many of those provided by the trusts of wealthy benefactors. In proportion, the less well-off have always proved more benevolent than the rich, and a little encouragement has consistently produced a remarkable and heartening response.

In a world of goodwill, where selling is the name of the game, it must surely be possible for a few industrial giants to take the initiative to encourage and help the vast numbers of genuinely kind people who would welcome the example and the guidance. In human terms, just 1 per cent of their profits would shatter the records of any financial index.

In the time it has taken the average reader to read this short chapter, forty people have died of starvation.

Closing Thoughts

*Those whom the gods wish to destroy they
first make millionaires.*

Amos Hargraves Jnr

In the stories of the celestial world, where the scales of
justice and human kindness measure the price for Eternity,
there is no reference to money. Sometimes there is little
understanding, as in the case of the righteous spectator who
watched at the Entrance to Heaven. There, he was unable to
control his distress when a priest was admitted without due
deference and yet the trumpeters of the Holy Kingdom
assembled to welcome a millionaire. It was the Angel at the
Gate who explained: 'We have many thousands of priests
here, but this is the first time a millionaire has been admitted.'

The divine worship of the Golden Calf throughout time
inspired the masses to honour the wealthy, and prompted
men like Calvin Coolidge to equate civilization with money.
In the days before caviar, man was content to pray for his
daily bread and a reserved seat in Paradise. Such devotions
brought comfort and contentment to the poor, but those
with affluent aspirations made their spiritual petitions for
greater returns on earth. And so it was when a frustrated
entrepreneur entered a church to seek assistance from the
Almighty in raising a substantial loan. About to plead his
case he became aware of a little man praying desperately for
£10. He immediately invited the man outside and handed
him a ten-pound note. Returning to his pew, he raised his
eyes towards heaven and prayed, 'Now, God, can I please
have your undivided attention?'

The problem of money is not so much its value but its
price. The respect it generates, the glamour it creates, and
the envy it provokes cannot be evaluated against the time it
consistently monopolizes. Multimillionaire Paul Getty is
credited with having said, 'Only the poor have the time to

count their blessings. In the oil business, time is money.' As Getty never smiled, his listeners believed he was voicing his philosophy.

At least in the fields of science, literature, music and the arts, the great are still respected regardless of their fortunes. There remains a distinction in attitudes towards those who dedicate their lives to amassing wealth and towards others, financially fortunate, who spend their precious years giving to society what is often priceless. Nobody cares whether Yehudi Menuhin is a millionaire, because he brought so much pleasure to so many; similarly with great medical practitioners who are able to extend the happy days of men on earth.

In an attempt to quantify medical advice the eminent surgeon and humorist, Dickson Wright, related the story of the specialist who counselled his worried patient, 'Cut out smoking, drinking and women.'

'How much longer will I live?' asked the patient.

'You won't,' came the response, 'but it will seem much longer.'

And so it is with those besotted with their fortunes who are suddenly faced with the prospect of leaving it all behind when they go. Perhaps the moment of truth hits hardest when they realize that neither their cheques nor their credit cards are worth taking with them.

As they step hopefully into the great beyond, such thoughts never haunt the poor.

ONCE IT COST ...

1945   A four-bedroomed house in a good suburb of North-West London cost £1,000.

1946   A headmaster of a grammar school could expect an annual salary of £700.

1947   A night for two at the Savoy Hotel cost £3 6s. (£3.30).

1948   A first-class return rail fare for a twenty-mile journey cost 5s. (25p).

1949   A weekend in a first-class hotel in Bournemouth with full board cost £4.

1950   A new Rolls-Bentley cost £2,000.

1951   A three-piece suit made by a private tailor cost £18.

1952   A package skiing holiday to St Moritz for two weeks, including hotel with full board, ski hire and daily skiing lessons, cost £32.

1953   Lunch for two at the Ritz, including a bottle of white wine, would cost £3.

1954   A week in the London Clinic, then London's foremost private hospital, cost £21.

1955   A visit to a private dentist cost 15s. (75p).

1956   Beef was 1/6 (8p) a pound.
             Eggs 4/6 (23p) a dozen.
             Butter 2/- (10p) a pound.
             Potatoes 2/4 (12p) for seven pounds.
             Whisky £1 16s (£1.80) a bottle.

1957   20 cigarettes cost 4s. (20p).

1958   A return night-flight to Paris cost £10.

1959   A night for two in a luxury suite at Claridge's cost
             £17.

1960   A new Humber Hawk cost £985.

1961   Dinner for two in a good-class suburban
             restaurant cost £2.00, including wine.

1962   Two seats in the stalls of a West End theatre cost
             £2.

1963   A salary of £4,000 a year enabled a married man
             to buy a comfortable six-roomed house in
             London, employ an au pair, have a good holiday
             abroad and send two children to fee-paying
             schools.

1964   An experienced secretary, based in London, could
             expect a salary of £600 a year.

1965   A full colonel in the British Army was paid £64 a
             day.

1966   A detached, double-fronted house in a good
             London suburb with 5 bedrooms, 3 reception
             rooms, 2 bathrooms, and a double garage, cost
             £20,000.

GLOSSARY

AAA
American term for corporations of the highest rating such as IBM, General Motors. UK companies, like ICI, GEC and Land Securities would enjoy that status.

Act of God
Expression in the insurance industry to describe a calamity or loss for which no machinery or individual is responsible, for example, lightning, a volcanic eruption, an earthquake.

Actuary
A financial specialist usually retained by insurance companies, pension funds or those concerned with longevity tables. They make precise calculations related to life expectations. For instance, it was actuaries who revised life-assurance premium rates for diabetics when the discovery of insulin prolonged the lives of sufferers of this illness.

Agent
An intermediary normally acting for one principal. (*See also* Lloyd's.)

AGM
Annual General Meeting. It is obligatory for every limited company to hold a meeting of its shareholders once a year.

Annuity
An income usually purchased from an insurance company for a given period or for life. Terms vary considerably depending on the age and sex of the annuitant and on whether the income is required immediately or at an agreed later date.

Assessor
A person retained by underwriters or others concerned with calculating the value of a loss. It might be said, in cases of housebreaking, that

	his prime concern is to ensure that the claimant makes roughly the same profit as the fence.
Asset	Actual value. A company may have total assets including stock, machinery and goodwill, with values calculated by its directors. Its net would refer to that which is readily marketable, namely its break-up value, e.g. cash and liquidation values.
Assurance	Originally a term used to describe the business of providing policies for events that will definitely occur – death, for instance. Latterly such companies also issue policies covering other catastrophes.
Averaging	Stockbroking term usually referring to buying further shares after a fall in price in the hope that an eventual rise will increase the profit. Also applies where shares are bought or sold over a period.
Bank	A business authorized by the Bank of England to accept money, provide loans, guarantees, letters of credit and other financial services. In recent years banks have tended to indulge in offering any legal service related to money.
Bank guarantee	An undertaking by a bank to meet a debt or deficiency should a company or individual be unable to do so. Such guarantees are normally given against adequate security. It is often convenient to obtain a guarantee rather than dispose of quoted securities or other assets.
Bank, merchant	Banks usually identified with serving companies and industries in such areas as takeovers, financial participation and investment programming.
Bargain	Another name for a stock exchange contract for the purchase or sale of shares.
Base rate	Normally the minimum rate at which banks and institutions operate in the money market. Most loans are made at base rate plus a percentage: for example, ICI may borrow at base plus 1 per

cent, but an individual could well be charged base rate plus 4 per cent. ICI can look after themselves but individuals should shop around.

Bears   Those who believe that an investment, a share or a particular financial market is on the way down. (Opposite of Bulls.)

Bonus   Life-insurance term to describe amount added to value of with-profit policies. Once credited, companies are obliged to pay them when policies mature or add their discounted value if policies are surrendered earlier.

Break-up   Companies and blocks of properties are sometimes said to be broken up, on the basis that the aggregate value of the parts can be greater than the apparent value of the whole.

Broker   An intermediary acting for more than one principal.

Bulls   Opposite of Bears. Those who believe that the share market or a particular investment will rise in value.

Capital Gains Tax   A tax introduced in the 1965 Finance Act. It is a tax on the appreciation of assets other than one's personal home, charities, Government Securities held for more than a year and National Savings Certificates. The tax relief is inflation-linked, and in 1986 affected capital gains in excess of £6,000 in any one year.

Capital Transfer Tax   Until the Finance Act of 1986, a tax payable on assets transferred during one's lifetime or on death. It replaced Estate Duty which was described as a tax extracted by the government from those too deeply involved to object. In an amended form, it is now covered by Inheritance Tax.

Chartist   Normally an investment consultant who believes that historical charts showing the movement of shares are indicative of future performance. In practice, such charts have proved useful and informative but often far from conclusive. The timing of buying and selling signals which charts indicate are best left to professionals to interpret. They can afford to make more mistakes.

Commission   Usually a remuneration related to the value of sale of goods or services. Such a financial arrangement is invariably expressed in percentage terms and agreed in advance.

Commodities   Assets other than shares or property which are readily marketable. Goods like coffee, cocoa, silver, copper and gold are traded in commodity exchanges where most substantial deals are transacted. Investment in this sector is generally considered speculative.

Compound   Investments which reflect growth and interest; rarely pay out any income although such income is liable for tax. In a non-growth investment compound interest would indicate that every year the interest is allowed to accumulate in order to attract further interest.

Discount   A reduction given in the normal market price.

Dividend cover   This term is frequently used to indicate the strength of the dividend currently paid by a company, and shows the number of times the net earnings actually cover the dividend paid. It is interesting to note that the dividends on the ordinary shares of companies like Shell may be covered two or three times but their preference dividends could be covered as much as a thousand times.

Dow Jones   The New York Stock Exchange equivalent to the *Financial Times* Index. It is an indication of the upward and downward movements of a basket of the major quoted securities. It does not necessarily affect the share prices of small companies but is a market barometer.

Endowment   The term is sometimes given to a large fund established for charitable purposes. Normally it

	relates to a life-insurance policy where the sum insured (with or without profits) is guaranteed to be paid on death or at the end of a given number of years. The minimum term is usually ten years.
Equities	The name given to shares participating in profits. The term equity also applies to the remaining value of an asset after deduction of loans, mortgages and other charges.
Estate Duty	Death duty tax replaced in the 1975 Finance Act by Capital Transfer Tax. The latter also applies, on a reduced scale, to gifts above a certain level made in one's lifetime.
Ex-gratia	A payment made more as an act of conscience or where there is genuine doubt as to whether the recipient has legal entitlement. Insurance companies frequently make ex-gratia payments where they accept that an insured believed he was protected by a policy even though the terms of the contract were explicitly to the contrary.
Exchange controls	Legislation which limits the movement of money from one country to another. Introduced in England in the Second World War, it was abolished in 1979. Labour parties, in opposition, have frequently threatened to re-introduce such controls if they are re-elected to power.
Executor	A person or institution nominated in a will to accept responsibility for its implementation.
FT Index	The *Financial Times* Indices are used to indicate the movement of the share market. There are three, comprising 30, 740 and 1,000 shares and the average variation is usually calculated on an hourly basis.
Friendly Societies	Established to provide mutual benefits, such as burial moneys, life assurance, etc. They prospered mostly in industrial areas.
Futures	A term largely used in the commodity market

to refer to a contract for delivery of assets at some future date.

Gilts

Gilt-Edged Securities are those guaranteed by the British government. The term is sometimes used to describe an investment where there is absolutely no risk. An undertaking given by a major bank or institution might well be described in this way.

Gross

A financial figure usually indicating that tax or other charges have not been deducted, e.g., Gross personal income usually means before deduction of tax.

Inflation

Rise in prices due to overall cost of a cross-section of consumer goods. Inflation-linked pensions, which are only enjoyed by certain categories of civil servants, have long been a contentious subject.

Lloyd's

International insurance market based in the City of London.

Agent. Underwriting Agents represent underwriting Members of Lloyd's, who are grouped into syndicates. (Another category is the Names Agent who is not attached to any syndicate, his business being to find Names for syndicates.)

Name. An underwriting Member of Lloyd's — in the risk business up to his last penny.

Syndicate. Run by underwriting Agents, these are groups of up to as many as 1,500 underwriting Members of Lloyd's.

Underwriter. Attached to a syndicate, he is the man who accepts or refuses risks on behalf of the Names forming the syndicate. By virtue of being a member of that syndicate, the underwriter is also an underwriting Member.

Underwriting Member. Known as a Name; each is represented by an Agent and is a member of, usually, a number of syndicates.

Minority interest

A share of an asset or holding of shares which does not give control and very often does not carry any influence.

Names   *See* Lloyd's.

Net asset value   The figure reached after deducting all interest and charges from the gross asset value. In making such assessments, careful investors often make further reductions in respect of old items of stock or machinery.

Premium   An amount paid to an insurance company to secure protection or a form of saving including life assurance. The term also describes an additional payment made for an asset over and above its market value. A property investor, knowing that it will enable him to develop the site, might well pay a substantial premium for a shop property.

Recovery stock   The shares of a company which, having fallen, are expected to rise again.

Risk   The amount that could be lost. An investor may instruct his stockbroker to sell a share at a particular price in order to limit his risk or alternatively quantify his gain. Material or health risks are mostly coverable by insurance.

Surrender   To cash in endowment or other life policy prior to the term for which the policy was effected.

Tax haven   Description given to a territory which has tax advantages over and above those in one's own country. Transfers of funds and assets to such areas are constantly under the scrutiny of the Inland Revenue Authorities.

Term assurance   A fixed-period life-assurance policy. It has no saving or investment content and is effected normally simply to provide capital on death within a given number of years. A cheap and effective form of protection.

Underwriters   In the stock market such people are obliged to acquire shares of a new company that are not purchased by the public. For this they receive a fee. In the insurance world, the underwriter actually accepts the risk on behalf of an insurance company or a syndicate of Members of Lloyd's. (*See also* Lloyd's.)

Will   A legally enforceable document which an
                  individual prepares concerning the distribution
                  of his assets on death.

Yield   The return on an investment. Shares are
                  purchased yielding a specific income based on
                  the last dividend declared. A future yield can be
                  calculated where it is known that income will
                  rise — for instance, in the case of an agreed
                  increase in the rent of a property.

INDEX